Lancashire

Who Lies Beneath?

Elizabeth Ashworth

D1340991

COUNTRYSIDE BOOKS
NEWBURY BERKSHIRE

First published 2009
© Elizabeth Ashworth 2009

COUNTRYSIDE BOOKS
3 Catherine Road
Newbury, Berkshire

To view our complete range of books,
please visit us at
www.countrysidebooks.co.uk

ISBN 978 1084674 167 8

Cover picture supplied by
Peter W. Joslin

Designed by Peter Davies, Nautilus Design

Produced through MRM Associates Ltd., Reading
Printed by Information Press, Oxford

Contents

Introduction

Whilst I was researching for my previous book, *Tales of Old Lancashire*, I came across the grave of the Childe of Hale and it reminded me of my father taking me to see the giant's grave in the cemetery at Blackburn. I did some research to see if I could find it again and discovered that the overgrown plot was now a neatly kept grave, with a recent headstone to keep alive the memory of Frederick John Kempster.

I then began to wonder what other interesting stories there might be connected with the places where people are buried. I'd known about the ancient rock-hewn graves at Heysham for many years. I'd visited the memorial to the Pretoria Pit disaster whilst writing about Westhoughton for a local magazine, and I also knew about the grave of Alice Nutter at Newchurch in Pendle.

Gradually, the idea for this book began to form in my mind and, with my camera and notebook in my hand, I began to wander around old churchyards and town cemeteries. I found burials that were ancient and those that were relatively recent. I found the brave, the good, the bad and the tragic.

I talked to people and asked them if they knew any interesting stories and was told about John T. Alker, who was 'killed by electricity'. I discovered heroes like the men of the St Annes lifeboat and Wallace Hartley who was the bandleader on the *Titanic*. I learnt about Margaret Clitherow who died horrifically for her faith. I read about the children of Freckleton who were victims of a Second World War aeroplane disaster, and I visited the graves of those who spent their lives helping others, like the Whitworth doctors.

The research was saddening at times but was always fascinating, and I was inspired by the lives of many of these people who deserve to be remembered and have their stories told. I hope you enjoy reading about them and maybe visiting some of the places where they now lie.

Elizabeth Ashworth

Acknowledgements

I would like to thank several people who have assisted me in the research for this book including Michael Finney for telling me about the grave of John T. Alker and for the use of his research; Mr Russell Brown, Mr Peter Moran and the Lancashire Aircraft Investigation Team for additional information about the Freckleton air disaster; and my son Ben for spending so many of his days off wandering around graveyards with me.

BLACKBURN

FREDERICK KEMPSTER: A GIANT OF A MAN

In Blackburn cemetery on Whalley New Road, you will find the grave of Frederick John Kempster, familiar to generations of children as the giant's grave. If you go into the cemetery at the top entrance, just off the ring road, and walk down the path you will see the grave straight in front of you.

He was born in 1889 in Bayswater, London, the fifth and youngest child of George and Florence Kempster, though his father died when Frederick was still young. Frederick quickly outgrew the rest of the family even though his brother George was recorded as being 6 ft 2 in, and one sister Rachel was also over 6 ft tall. By the age of 19, Frederick had reached 7 ft 4 in, which must have been an asset when he played in goal for the Silvertown Rubber Works Football Club.

After leaving school his trade was as a basket maker, but his hands became so large that he found it difficult to wield normal tools. For a time he lived with his sister Rachel and brother-in-law James Rayner – who was a gardener – in Avebury, Wiltshire. He lived in a house that was partly made from an upturned boat because he was unable to stand upright in most rooms.

Here he became known for performing a variety of tricks including shaking hands with people through upstairs windows, passing an old penny coin through the ring he wore on his finger and lighting his cigarette from gas lamps on the street. A friend, Henry Lawes, had an early Ford motor car and he would take the top off so that Fred could sit in the back and be driven around the countryside. He had a reputation for his kind and friendly nature and was said to be upset if children, whom he loved, were ever afraid of him.

Such was the fascination with Frederick that he took up a career as an attraction in fairs that went all over the country. As a result of his travels, he became known not only as the Blackburn Giant but also as Fred the Giant of Wiltshire, the Melksham Giant, the Gentle Essex Giant and the Giant of Weston Village.

In 1910 he joined the circus in Blackpool and went to Germany where he was billed as 'Frederick the Great – the English Giant'. His huge vest was hung outside the fairground booth as an attraction. He also appeared with the giantess Brunnhilde, who was four inches taller than him.

When the First World War began he was classed as a 'security risk' by the Germans and was kept in an internment camp between 1914 and 1916. He fell ill during his second week as a Prisoner of War and was hospitalised until the American Ambassador in Berlin persuaded the Germans to release him. He came home emaciated, round-shouldered and was never in good health again. In 1917 he was admitted to a hospital in London for a nervous complaint and it was here that one morning, owing to a misunderstanding, he ate the breakfast intended for the whole ward. It was said that for him a normal breakfast consisted of four loaves and six eggs.

In 1918 he came to Blackburn with the Easter Fair, lodging at the Haymarket Hotel. He contracted influenza which turned to pneumonia and had to be admitted to hospital. However, this turned out to be no easy task. He had to be carried from the hotel to the ambulance by eight men and, as he couldn't fit on a stretcher, they had to use a fireman's jump sheet to transport him. Then, when they got him into the ambulance, they found that Fred had to pull his knees up to his chin to allow them to shut the

The last resting place of the British Giant

doors. He was admitted to Queen's Park Hospital in Blackburn, via the fire escape, and he needed three beds pushed together. Sadly he died there on 15th April 1918, at the age of 29.

Ten tons of earth were dug for his grave. Ten pallbearers carried his coffin and fourteen men were needed to lower it. The coffin was 9 ft long. With its brass mountings and shroud, it cost £9, at a time when the average price was around £4. The undertaker, Mr Walker, recorded his height as 8 ft 4½ in, which would make him Britain's tallest ever man. He weighed 27 stone and wore size 22 shoes.

His funeral took place on 19th April and attracted a large crowd. For many years afterwards, children would take flowers to his long grave. Although the giant's grave has always been something of a legend in the town it had been neglected over the years until a booklet about Frederick Kempster's life was written by Colin Alexander-Jones.

Now it is neat and tidy and there is a recent headstone with the inscription:

IN AFFECTIONATE REMEMBRANCE OF
FREDERICK JOHN KEMPSTER
(THE BRITISH GIANT)
DIED APRIL 15TH 1918
AGED 29 YEARS
GONE BUT NOT FORGOTTEN BY BILLY

BOLTON

Samuel Crompton: inventor of the spinning mule

The grave of Samuel Crompton can be found near the main door of St Peter's parish church at Bolton, not far from the centre of the town. There is a large granite monument, erected in 1861 by local textile workers, on which an inscription reads:

Beneath this stone are interred the mortal remains of Samuel Crompton, of Bolton, late of Hall i' th' Wood, in the township of Tonge, inventor of the Spinning Machine called the Mule; who departed this life on the 26th day of June 1827, aged 72 years. 'Mors Ultimo Linea Rerum Est.'

The Latin means: 'Death is the last boundary of human affairs'.

Samuel Crompton was born on 3rd December 1753, at Firwood Fold, into a farming family who also produced a small quantity of cloth by spinning and weaving first wool and, later, cotton on spindles and looms in their own home. The family struggled to make a living on the farm which had once belonged to them but had been mortgaged by Samuel's grandfather and sold by his father who subsequently lived there as a tenant. Soon after Samuel's birth the family moved from the farm to live at Hall-i'-th'-Wood in Bolton as caretakers.

When Samuel was five his father died, leaving his mother to bring up Samuel and his two younger sisters, as well as care for his disabled uncle, Alexander Crompton. As soon as Samuel was old enough he was expected to spin and weave to supplement the family's income, although his mother did manage to send Samuel to be educated at the school of Mr Lever in Church Street.

By the time he was fourteen, Samuel was using the Spinning Jenny that had recently been invented by James Hargreaves and could spin eight spindles at once. But he found that the thread often broke and he was increasingly frustrated by having to stop to mend the yarn. He began to wonder if he could find a better method of spinning the cotton to make it stronger.

He was good at making things and, following his father's interest in music, he had already succeeded in making a violin and teaching himself to play. He joined the Bolton orchestra where he earned 18 pence a night, which he used to buy tools to construct a new spinning machine. He worked on his invention from the age of twenty-two for five years, labouring into the night. The neighbours began to wonder if Hall-i'-th'-Wood was haunted, as they heard strange noises and saw lights burning at all hours. Samuel also had to work in secret, since he feared that the Luddites might break in and destroy his work. He was so afraid that in one of the rooms he made a trap door so that his invention could be taken apart and hoisted into the roof space for safety.

The impressive memorial to Samuel Crompton

At first his invention was called the Hall-i'-th'-Wood wheel, but it later gained the nickname of the 'Mule' as it was a cross between the Spinning Jenny and the fully mechanised spinning machine that had been produced by Richard Arkwright from Preston, with the help of John Kay, a clockmaker from Warrington. The 'Mule' managed to imitate the actions of the hand-spinner by pulling and stretching the cotton, as well as twisting it into a thread. This meant a much stronger and finer thread could be spun, resulting in the production of high-quality cotton cloth in Lancashire which rivalled the muslin imported from India.

Once the machine was complete and yarn was being produced, the secret was out. The first yarn sold at Bolton market caused a sensation and Crompton and his wife, Mary Pimlott, who was also adept at spinning, were kept very busy. However, they were plagued by people who wanted to discover the secret of the machine and who tried to peer through the window to see the spinning process. It is said that some even climbed ladders to look through upstairs windows and that Samuel had to work behind a screen.

Richard Arkwright, himself, even paid Samuel a visit. Arkwright's efforts to mechanise the production of cotton meant that more of the textile industry was moving from cottages into factories and he could have given

Samuel some business advice but, unfortunately, Samuel was out when he called. However, Samuel wasn't interested in business and he couldn't afford to patent the machine anyway; he just wanted to make a living.

In the end, he was so fed up with being pestered and spied on that he turned to Mr Pilkington, a Bolton manufacturer, for advice – and his advice was that Samuel should give his invention away! Not only did he give away the secret of its workings, he actually gave away the machine he was working on in return for a promise that 80 firms and individual manufacturers would pay a fee, which totalled just over £67. Of this he only ever received around £50 – about enough money to allow him to build another Mule for his own use. He then moved his family to a farmhouse at Sharples in an attempt to gain some peace and privacy, and whilst he grew poorer the cotton industry grew richer on his invention.

Sir Robert Peel, 1st Baronet, who had a calico printing firm at Church, near Accrington, tried to help. He offered him a highly paid job with his firm, but Samuel refused, partly because he valued his independence and partly because he believed that Peel had insulted him on an earlier visit by offering money to compensate for the time Samuel had spent showing him the Mule.

In the end he was reduced to such poverty that the firms who were using his Mule eventually agreed to make him a yearly payment of £63 pounds, but he was only paid twice before he died in 1827. Thirty-five years later the people of Bolton decided to erect a statue in his memory. It cost £2,000.

BOLTON-BY-BOWLAND

RALPH PUDSAY: A FAMILY MAN IN ARMOUR

Ralph Pudsay is buried in a magnificent tomb in the church of St Peter and St Paul at Bolton-by-Bowland. The top of the Craven limestone tomb is engraved with depictions of Sir Ralph in full armour with his three wives and 25 children – and if you look carefully you will see a Roman numeral in the skirts of each wife that represents how many children she bore. His first wife Matilda Tempest had two children, his second Margaret Tunstall had six and his third Edwina gave birth to 17 children. All 25 children are named on the tomb and each picture is different.

Bolton-by-Bowland is a picturesque village high in the Ribble Valley which appears in the Domesday Book as Bodeton, meaning an enclosure with dwellings. There has been a church here since around 1190. The first mention of the Pudsay family name was when Simon de Pudsay married Katherine, the daughter of Richard de Bolton, in 1312. The Pudsays remained in the village at Bolton Hall which they extended and improved over the centuries until the death of Bridget Pudsay in 1770.

It was at Bolton Hall that Sir Ralph Pudsay gave shelter to Henry VI in 1464. After his defeat by the Yorkists during the Wars of the Roses, Henry spent many months hiding out in what is now Cumbria and Lancashire, though Bolton-by-Bowland was at that time in the West Riding of Yorkshire. He may have come here because Sir Ralph was married to Margaret Tunstall and her father, Sir Thomas Tunstall, was an esquire of the body to the king. Sir Thomas's own residence at Thurland Castle was in danger and he may have seen Bolton Hall as a safer place for the king and himself to hide out.

During the year that he lived here it is said that Henry discovered a natural spring by dowsing. He had a well dug at the spot and a bath-house built so that he could take cold baths. The well, which is on private land, is still known as King Henry's Well.

There is also a theory that when Sir Ralph enlarged the church nave and had a tower built, the king was responsible for the design of the tower which

The Pudsay tomb at Bolton-by-Bowland

appears to be more sophisticated than those of other churches in the area.

CHIPPING

LIZZIE DEAN: HER LAST WISH THWARTED

To the south-east of the church of St Bartholomew at Chipping, underneath the ancient yew tree, is the grave of Lizzie Dean. The inscription reads:

> *Sacred to the memory of Elizabeth Dean*
> *who departed this life Nov 5th 1835*
> *in the 20th year of her age.*
> *'There is a hallowed sweetness in*
> *cherishing a remembrance of those we loved.'*

If you came across the grave by accident you might wonder how this young girl had died; but if you also discovered that when she was buried her grave was in unconsecrated ground your curiosity would increase.

Elizabeth Dean worked at the Sun Inn just across the road from the church. Legend tells that she was pretty, liked to wear bright colours and that many of the young lads from the village thought her very attractive. She caught the eye of one in particular, and keen to have his way with her he promised her marriage. The promise was false though and it wasn't long before he began to deceive her with another girl, reputed to be Lizzie's best friend. He promised this girl marriage too, but this time it seems he was serious and went through with the ceremony.

Poor Lizzie slept in the attic room at the

Lizzie Dean's grave at Chipping

pub which looks out over the churchyard. One morning she woke to the ringing of bells and looked out of the window to witness her lover coming out of the church with his new wife. In anguish and despair she wrote a suicide note and hanged herself.

The note, which was found clutched in her hand, asked for her body to be buried near the path that led to the church door so that every Sunday her lover and his wife would have to walk past her grave. But this was not possible. Suicides could not be buried in consecrated ground and Lizzie was buried around the back of the church where she still lies, and where many people must pass by her grave without noticing it. But it is there for you to visit it and contemplate the cruelty of the unnamed man who betrayed her.

Many people who have lived in or visited the Sun Inn at Chipping claim to have seen Lizzie's ghost haunting the pub. She has been described as a 'colourful female figure with brown hair in ringlets and a dress that looked like it had been in a washing machine many times and the colours had mingled'. Perhaps she haunts the pub because her last wish was not carried out?

CLIVIGER

JAMES SCARLETT: LEADER OF THE CHARGE OF THE HEAVY BRIGADE

Sir James Yorke Scarlett is buried in the churchyard of St John's at Holme Chapel, Cliviger between Burnley and Todmorden. His grave can be found near the church door on the left as you walk up the path from the road. He was the leader of the lesser-known of the two cavalry charges at the battle of Balaclava in the Crimean War – not the charge of the Light Brigade, but the earlier, successful, charge of the Heavy Brigade.

Born in 1799 he was the second son of James Scarlett, the first Baron Abinger. He was educated at Eton and Trinity College, Cambridge before attending Sandhurst. He was briefly engaged in politics when he became a Conservative MP for Guildford from 1836 to 1841, and in 1840 was promoted to command his regiment, the 5th Dragoon Guards.

In 1854, at the age of 55, he was on the verge of retiring into civilian life when the war with Russia began and he was appointed as the commander of the Heavy Brigade. He sailed for Turkey and arrived at Varna, where many men were sick with cholera, then towards the end of September 1854 he arrived in the Crimea.

Early in the morning of 25th October a force of around 25,000 Russians began to threaten the English camp near Balaclava. Brigadier Scarlett (later promoted to General) received orders from Lord Raglan to move from the rear of the army to an important tactical point at Kadikoi. But as they marched Scarlett saw the enemy coming over the top of the Causeway Heights with the intention of making an attack. He didn't know how many Russians there were, but they actually numbered around 3,000 whilst Scarlett had only about 800 men. However, he told his left column, which consisted of around 300 sabres – swordsmen on horseback – of the Royal Scots Greys and the Inniskillin Dragoons to 'wheel around' and face the enemy, then gave them orders to attack uphill.

With Scarlett leading the way the men charged and immediately engaged with the enemy. After a few moments their charge was supported by the men from the remaining squadrons. Scarlett rode into the midst of the fight, slashing left and right with his sword, and although he was covered in bruises and minor cuts he escaped without any serious injury; however, the top of his massive brass helmet had been caved in by one powerful blow from an adversary. In all, 20 British soldiers died in the charge, but 200 Russians were killed and the survivors, perhaps thinking that another charge was imminent, withdrew.

Although Tennyson's poem about the charge of the Light Brigade is well known he also wrote a poem that commemorates the charge of the Heavy Brigade. It records the charge of the 'gallant three hundred' who charged uphill to attack 'thousands of Russians gathered there on the height' and tells how Scarlett's men 'drove thro' the midst of the foe' who had surrounded them and 'drove it in wild disarray ... up the hill, up the hill, up the hill, out of the field, and over the brow and away'.

But later in the day came the charge of the Light Brigade. Although it is sometimes remembered as an act of selfless bravery it was more probably a military blunder that cost 350 lives in just twenty minutes. When the survivors returned Brigadier Scarlett tried to secure some advantage from the slaughter. At the head of his dragoons he led a second charge down the valley of death, but Lord Lucan, his commander, called a halt and later told

General Sir James Yorke Scarlett's last resting place

him: 'I have lost the Light Brigade; I will not lose the Heavy Brigade too if I can help it.' Scarlett thought that if he had been allowed to continue he could have captured and carried off the twelve Russian guns at the head of the valley. For his services at Balaclava he was promoted to the rank of major-general and in 1855 he was created a KCB.

James Scarlett returned to England but he was offered the post of the commander of the entire British cavalry in the Crimea and the rank of lieutenant-general, and despite his family's reluctance for him to return there, he did so without delay.

At the end of the war he was appointed to command the cavalry in the Aldershot district and was made commander of the Aldershot camp. He was invested as a Knight Grand Cross, Order of the Bath (GCB) in 1869 and on 1st November 1870 he retired from active duty.

It may seem strange that such a well-known soldier and a hero of the Crimean War is buried in a small Lancashire churchyard, especially when the Royal Garrison Church at Aldershot has a bronze bust of Scarlett flanked by two full-sized bronze cavalry troopers of his former regiments, and there is also a plaque in his memory on the choir stalls in the Royal Garrison church at Plymouth. However, he was married to Charlotte Anne, the daughter and heiress of Colonel Hargreaves of Burnley, and he returned to live at Bank Hall in Burnley after his retirement. There he renewed his interest in politics and stood for election in Burnley but was defeated by the Liberal candidate.

He died suddenly on 6th December 1871 at the age of 72. Charlotte died on 9th February 1888, at the age of 82, and is buried in the same grave.

COLNE

WALLACE HARTLEY: NEARER, MY GOD, TO THEE

In the cemetery at Colne you will find the grave of Wallace Hartley who was drowned at sea when the *Titanic* sank in 1912. Go straight down the main central path and the grave is near the bottom on the left-hand side, just set back from the path. It is a tall white monument engraved with the words:

'In Loving Memory of Wallace Henry, the beloved son of Albion and Elizabeth Hartley, formerly of Colne, who lost his life in the S.S. Titanic Disaster on April 15th 1912, aged 33 years, and was interred on May 18th 1912.'

A violin is also carved into the gravestone and there is a page from Arthur Sullivan's setting of the hymn *Nearer, My God, To Thee*, the hymn tune which was reputedly played by the band of which Wallace Hartley was the leader, as the ship sank.

Wallace Henry Hartley was born on 2nd June 1878, at 92 Greenfield Road in Colne. His parents Albion and Elizabeth were textile workers and he had an elder sister Mary Ellen and a younger sister Lizzie. A younger brother died in infancy.

He was a talented violinist and as he came from a musical family his father had always encouraged his talent. When he left school Wallace Hartley went to work as a clerk in the local Craven and Union bank and stayed there until he moved with the family to Huddersfield in 1895. There he joined the Huddersfield Philharmonic Orchestra as a violinist whilst continuing to work as a bank clerk during the day.

It wasn't until 1903 that he first performed professionally when he moved to the seaside town of Bridlington, where he played first violin in the Bridlington Municipal Orchestra. In 1909 he began his career as a musician

Wallace Hartley's grave in Colne cemetery

on board the Cunard liners that sailed between the UK and USA. He played on the *Lucania*, the *Lusitania*, playing second violin in the ship's five-man band, and in October 1910 he was promoted to bandmaster on the *Mauretania*, which was the best and fastest ship afloat at the time.

When the new White Star Line's ship *Titanic* sailed from Southampton on 10th April 1912 Wallace Hartley was the bandmaster. He had been reluctant to accept the job as he had just proposed to Maria Robinson, and was considering giving up working on the ships to be with her. But not only was this a promotion, it also meant a pay rise and, hoping that the voyage would provide him with contacts for future work, he agreed to go.

On 10th April 1912, Wallace Hartley and his band played on the upper deck of the ship as the first class passengers embarked. The *Titanic* made good speed westwards across the Atlantic towards New York until there was a sighting of ice on Sunday 14th April. Hartley, who had crossed the Atlantic Ocean over 80 times, probably wasn't unduly concerned, but shortly after midnight, it became clear that the ship was sinking and passengers were directed to the lifeboats. Wallace assembled all the musicians to play in the first class lounge and as people waited to board lifeboats the band continued to play as if nothing was amiss. When passengers were moved onto the boat deck the musicians moved out too. Many people believe that their music helped to keep passengers calm and allowed the lifeboats to be loaded in an orderly fashion.

At 2.20 am on 15th April 1912, the *Titanic* sank and in the last wave to engulf the decks all eight bandsmen were swept into the icy waters and drowned.

Two weeks later Wallace Hartley's body was found floating in the Atlantic Ocean by the cable ship *Mackay-Bennett*. First recorded as body number 224, his identity was soon apparent. He was still clothed in his bandsman's uniform of brown overcoat, green facings, black boots and green socks. His music box was still strapped to his body and among the items found in his pockets was a gold fountain pen engraved with his initials – WHH.

His body, perhaps ironically, packed in ice to preserve it, was returned to the UK aboard the SS *Arabic* and he was brought home to Colne to a hero's welcome. Over 40,000 people lined the streets of the small town to pay their respects at his funeral on 18th May. The procession, almost half a mile long and led by seven bands, made its way to the Bethel Chapel where Wallace had sung in the choir as a boy. The congregation for the service totalled over 1,000, in a building designed only to hold 700. As he was buried an orchestra played *Nearer, My God, To Thee*.

There is also a memorial to Wallace Hartley on the main street in Colne that was erected in 1915. The plaque records that it was *'Erected by voluntary contributions to commemorate the heroism of a native of this town.'*

CRAWSHAWBOOTH

ROSSENDALE PET CEMETERY

High on the windswept hill above the village of Crawshawbooth, just outside Rawtenstall, is the Rossendale pet cemetery. The steep road beyond the old Quaker meeting house leads up to what must be one of the most interesting burial grounds in the county.

The Rossendale Pet Crematorium and Memorial Gardens were founded by Alan Dickinson in 1967. After the accidental death of his dog on the hillside, he buried his pet and erected a headstone to mark the grave. From this small tribute grew a burial ground for hundreds of pets including cats, dogs and even horses. A plaque commemorating Alan Dickinson's death at the age of 75 in 1997 stands next to a larger one to mark the official opening

The pet cemetery at Rossendale

of the gardens on 28th April 1971 by Martin Dobson, who was captain of Burnley Football Club and a member of the England International under-23 team.

The cemetery covers a 15-acre site looking across the Rossendale valley and offers pet owners the options of burial or cremation for their pets. The memorial gardens never close and pet owners and friends are welcome at any time.

The cemetery, which is the largest in Britain with over 1,500 graves, has its own crematorium and a licence for a number of people to be buried alongside their pets. Owners' ashes can be scattered on pets' graves, re-uniting them for eternity.

FORMBY

A SONGWRITER, THE FORMBY FAMILY AND A STRANGE STONE

Percy French

The grave of Percy French can be found in the churchyard at St Luke's, Formby. It is almost parallel with the west door of the church to the left

Percy French's grave at Formby

of the path and is regularly visited by his admirers, so don't be surprised to find a posy of bluebells in the springtime; they were his favourite flowers. Part of the inscription on the gravestone reads: *'So long thy power hath blest me, sure it still will lead me on: o'er moor and fen, o'er crag and torrent till night is gone.'*

William Percy French was born on 1st May 1854 at Clooniquin in County Roscommon in Ireland where there is an elaborate memorial to him near the site of his birthplace. He is remembered as a prolific writer of Irish comic songs as well as being a poet, entertainer and watercolour artist. He is possibly best known for the lyrics for the song *The Mountains O'Mourne*.

He was the second son of Christopher French, who was a Protestant landowner descended from one of the merchant tribes of Galway. His mother was Susan Emma, whose maiden name had been Percy – the name she gave him as a middle name and by which he became known professionally, though he was always called 'Willie' by his friends.

William Percy French was educated in England then went to Trinity College in Dublin in 1872 to study civil engineering but, instead of concentrating on his studies, he spent much of his time playing his banjo, writing songs and painting in watercolours. In 1877 he wrote a comic song called *Abdulla Bulbul Ameer* for a college concert. He later sold the song for £5 to a publisher and though it became a huge hit he received no further financial reward.

He eventually graduated in 1881 with an engineering qualification and was set to emigrate to Canada when he was offered a job on a government drainage scheme in County Cavan as what he called an 'inspector of drains'. It was here that as well as continuing to develop his musical skills he was inspired to paint landscapes, believing his true vocation was to be an artist. He was very talented, as the increase in the value of his work shows, though at the time he often gave paintings away to friends or in exchange for board and lodgings.

When there were staff cuts in County Cavan in 1887, French turned to journalism and became the editor of a weekly magazine called *The Jarvey* and used the opportunity to promote a series of concerts of his comic songs, such as *Phil the Fluter's Ball* and *Slattery's Mounted Fut* under the name of the Jarvey Concert Company. When the magazine folded he helped to write and take the leading role in two comic operas co-written with his friend Dr W. H. Collisson.

However there was sadness too when his wife Ettie (Ethel Armytage Moore, who was from Cavan) died in childbirth just one year and a day after their marriage; their baby daughter died a few weeks later. This led to some poignant writing such as *Gortnamona, Only Goodnight* and *Not Lost But Gone Before*.

He now abandoned both engineering and journalism and turned to the stage as a full-time career and became known professionally as W. Percy French. He wrote, produced and played a major part in a topical revue called *Dublin Up To Date* which consisted of songs, sketches, stories and caricatures. This show was the basis of all his future entertainment that led to his fame.

Another of his well-known songs was *Are Ye Right There Michael?* - a song that ridiculed the state of the rail system in rural County Clare and provoked the railway company into taking libel action against him. The case was apparently thrown out of court after French arrived late for the hearing and when questioned by the judge about his tardiness explained that he had travelled by the West Clare Railway.

In 1894 he married his second wife, Helen (Lennie) Sheldon of Burmington House, Warwickshire, and they had three daughters – Ettie (named after his first wife), Mollie and Joan. Joan, the last surviving daughter died in 1996.

By 1900 he had brought his talents to London. He played at music halls and theatres all over the country as well as touring the USA, Canada and the West Indies, though he never neglected the holiday resorts and towns of Ireland during the summer season.

He was taken ill whilst performing in Glasgow in 1920 and went to stay with his cousin, Canon Richardson, who was the vicar of Holy Trinity church in Formby, to recuperate. But his condition worsened and he died of pneumonia on 24th January. As the church of the Holy Trinity had no graveyard, Percy French was buried at St Luke's, which is adjacent to the nature reserve at Formby, where you can see a colony of wild red squirrels as you walk down to the sand dunes.

It is a lovely spot, though it is not Percy French's home so, to mark the 50th anniversary of his death, the Liverpool Irish Society added a block of Mourne granite to his grave inscribed: '*In Memory of a Well Loved Songwriter, Poet, Painter, Author and Entertainer. Ar Deis De Go Raib A Anam [May His Soul Be On The Right Hand of God]. Amen'*.

The Formby family

Near Percy French's grave you will notice a collection of tabletop graves.

The Formby family graves

These are the burials of members of the Formby family, the oldest of which is that of Richard Formby who died in 1737. Along with the Formby coat of arms it is inscribed *'An honest man and a good father'*. Nearby, his wife Mary, who died in 1766, has an epitaph on the end panel of her grave that refers to the last chapter of the book of Proverbs in the Bible. The verses relate to the good qualities of a wife and end: *'Many women are good wives, but you are the best of all of them'*.

The original church that stood here was known as Formby Chapel and was destroyed by a storm in 1739. Although the churchyard continued to be used for burials it was a later Richard Formby who gave the land where the present church was built in 1852. He trained as a doctor and worked in Liverpool where he experimented with early forms of anaesthesia. He chose St Luke as the patron saint of the new church as he too was a doctor.

An ancestor of his, also called Richard Formby, who lived in the late 14th century, was reputed to have grown to a gigantic height and went to court as armour bearer to King Henry IV. When he died in 1407, he was buried in York Minster. In 1829 a disturbed man by the name of Jonathan Martin set fire to the choir stalls and in the ensuing blaze a beam fell and landed on the grave, cracking the gravestone and exposing the bones beneath. These were measured and his height was verified as being 7 ft. One day when Richard Formby was in the minster, he saw the damaged gravestone of his ancestor. He provided a copy for York and brought the original gravestone back to Formby, where it now lies in the porch of St Luke's. The Latin inscription is translated as: *'Here lies Richard Formby at one time armour bearer to our Lord the King who died on 22nd of the month of September in the year of our lord 1407. To whose soul may God grant rest.'*

The Godstone

In the far corner of the graveyard, under the trees beyond the stocks, is a small stone that bears an unusual inscription. It is called the Godstone. No one seems to be sure exactly what it is. Some suggest that it was part of the old church building, others that it was a rebus – a type of pictorial explanation – that was used by missionaries to convert the Vikings to Christianity. It shows the steps that must be climbed (perhaps faith, hope and charity) to reach the cross (Christianity) and finally the reward of the circle at the top (heaven).

The Godstone in the churchyard
at St Luke's, Formby

Whatever its origins, it was a custom in times gone by to carry the bodies of the dead three times in an anti-clockwise direction around the Godstone to drive away any evil spirits before the burial.

FRECKLETON

Victims of an air disaster

In the Holy Trinity churchyard at Freckleton is a communal grave whose memorial reads:

> *Sacred to the memory of the two teachers, thirty-eight infant scholars and seven civilians who lost their lives when an American Liberator bomber crashed during a thunderstorm and destroyed a part of the adjoining school and other property on the 23rd August 1944. This monument was erected over their grave by public subscription.*
> *"In God We Trust"*

The day had dawned bright and sunny. At around half past ten in the morning, two classes of infants aged between four and six, some of whom had only begun school the day before, were at their lessons with their teachers at the Holy Trinity Church of England school in Freckleton.

About a mile away, at the former RAF Warton Aerodrome where 10,000 American servicemen were based to repair and maintain aircraft, two US B-24 Liberator bombers took off on a test flight. But the skies suddenly grew dark as a storm came rolling in off the Irish Sea and the control tower radioed the aircraft to return to base.

The thunderstorm came in fast and was fierce. The bright summer day turned to night and the rain was so heavy that witnesses said it was impossible to see across the road. The torrential downpour caused flash floods along the coast in Southport and Blackpool, waterspouts were seen in the Ribble estuary and a wind speed of almost 60 mph was recorded at Hutton meteorological station.

What happened next is not entirely clear but it seems that the pilot of one of the planes, 1st Lieutenant Pete Manassero, abandoned any attempt to land and decided to head north away from the worst of the weather. The second aircraft, piloted by 1st Lieutenant John Bloemendal, along with crew members T/Sgt James M. Parr and Sgt Gordon W. Kinney, continued to

The memorial to those who lost their lives in the Freckleton air disaster

be buffeted by the storm. The pilot fought against the elements in a battle which he just could not win. One eyewitness saw the aircraft struck by lightning. As the plane descended, out of control, it clipped the tops of trees before partly destroying three houses and the Sad Sack Café*. As it broke apart, one section of the 25-ton plane landed on the infants' classrooms. The building was quickly engulfed in a fireball as 2,700 gallons of fuel from the ruptured tanks burst into flames.

The clock in one classroom stopped at 10.47 am. Within 20 minutes the peaceful scene had been transformed into a disaster area.

Witnesses heard the screams as they ran through the torrential rain to help. Local people and young American airmen from the base pulled at the rubble with their bare hands in an attempt to find survivors. Seven children and two teachers were pulled out alive, but the teachers and four of the children later died from their burns and injuries; just three children survived. Although the older children, who were in another part of the school, were unhurt, they were left shocked and distraught.

Then, as quickly as the storm had come it was gone. The sun shone again, but the village would never be the same. The local policeman, PC Robert Nelson, who knew most of the children personally, was asked to cut off locks of hair from some of the victims, for parents to keep as mementoes. One mother whose daughter died that morning received a telegram only six days later telling her that her husband had been killed serving with the East Lancashire regiment in France.

In all, 38 infant school children, two teachers and another 24 civilians and airmen, including all three aircrew of the B-24 bomber died that summer morning. Some of the deaths were at the Sad Sack Café, which had been opened to cater for the Americans from the nearby base. Three British civilians, four RAF personnel and seven Americans were killed in the café.

Because of the sensitive nature of the story it was kept quiet at the time and it has been, perhaps, one of the best-kept secrets of the Second World War. For the rest of the country it had been a day of rejoicing as Paris had been liberated and the end of the war seemed not far off.

The official report into the crash said that the exact cause was unknown, although the pilot's underestimation of the violence of the storm may have been a contributory factor. They concluded that Lt Bloemendal had not fully realised the danger until he made his approach to land, by which time he had insufficient altitude and speed to manoeuvre given the violent winds and downdrafts he must have encountered.

The Americans paid for a lavish funeral for the dead and Brigadier General Isaac W. Ott, commander of the airbase, was ordered to represent the USAAF. The three US aircrew killed in the B-24 were buried in a US cemetery in the south of England and after the war their bodies were sent for reburial in their home states at the request of their families.

A fund was set up with the intention of building a memorial hall to commemorate the victims of the tragedy, though this was not finally opened until September 1977.

In August 1945 a memorial garden and children's playground was opened at Freckleton. A stone memorial is inscribed: *'This playground presented to the children of Freckleton by their neighbours of Base Air Depot No. 2 USAAF in recognition and remembrance of their common loss in the disaster of August 23rd 1944'*.

* Sad Sack was a cartoon character created by Sgt George Baker in a Second World War comic strip. Set in the USA, *Sad Sack* was a lowly private, experiencing some of the absurdities and humiliations of military life.

GISBURN

Francis Duckworth: a composer of hymns

Hidden in the long grass behind the church of St Mary the Virgin at Gisburn, you will find the grave of composer Francis Duckworth. Many people will be familiar with his hymn tune *Rimington*, named after the tiny village that nestles below Pendle where he was born on Christmas Day 1862. He was the fourth

Francis Duckworth's grave

son of Robert and Mary Ann Duckworth who kept the local grocery store and post office. He grew up to become a wholesale grocer in Colne and was also the organist at Albert Road Methodist church.

After the death of his wife in 1901 he found great solace in his music, in particular in the composition of hymn tunes. *Rimington* was sung for the first time at the Colne Whitsuntide processions in 1904. He later composed more tunes, eighteen of which were published in the *Rimington Hymnal*. He dedicated them to his daughter, Margaret, who sadly died at the age of 28 in 1917. You can see the names of the songs inscribed on the gravestone, together with the music for the opening of his most famous hymn tune.

GORTON

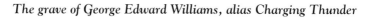

George Edward Williams: alias Charging Thunder

Buried in Gorton cemetery is George Edward Williams – and with a name like that no one would suspect that the man in the grave was born on the

The grave of George Edward Williams, alias Charging Thunder

prairies of Pine Ridge in South Dakota as a native American and that his original name was Charging Thunder.

He was one of the Lakota members of the Oglala tribe of the Sioux nation who were well known for their skills as horsemen, and who could count Sitting Bull and Crazy Horse amongst their number.

As a young man, Charging Thunder became part of a show which was brought to Europe by William Frederick Cody, better known as Buffalo Bill. Cody had previously worked as a US Army scout and as a tracker and buffalo hunter he had won the respect of the native Americans. However, when the buffalo herds were in danger of being wiped out because of over-hunting he turned to entertainment to make his living, creating *Buffalo Bill's Wild West Show*, which performed in America and also toured in Europe.

In November 1887, Buffalo Bill and his show arrived in Salford with 97 American Indians, 180 broncos, 18 buffalo, 14 mules and donkeys, ten elk and two deer. The show set up camp in tepees on the banks of the River Irwell, near to where Salford Quays and the Lowry now stand, and it thrilled the crowds with exhibitions of mock fights between 'cowboys and Indians', complete with stagecoaches and horses. There was room for 10,000 spectators and people came from miles around for a taste of the Wild West in Lancashire, with exhibitions of riding bucking broncos, roping, lassoing and many other skills.

In 1903, the show returned for a second time and now 26-year-old Charging Thunder was among the participants. He rode horses bareback, did handstands and jumped from horse to horse. It was whilst he was working for the show that he met Josephine, who was one of the American horse trainers. They fell in love, got married and decided to stay in Lancashire. They first set up home in Darwen, but later moved to West Gorton in Manchester. They had two daughters, Bessie and Gladys, and a son, George, and recently some of Charging Thunder's grandchildren have been traced to the Salford area.

When he registered his name with the British immigration authorities, Charging Thunder chose the name George Edward Williams. He worked for a time at Belle Vue Circus as a handyman and is said to have been particularly fond of the elephants and snakes. He later worked for a local engineering firm and as a doorman at the local cinema, where he became a well-known local character in the town.

He died of pneumonia at the age of 52 in 1929 and was buried at Gorton. His grave is at plot number 386 in the W section of the cemetery between a conifer and a large silver birch tree.

HAWKSHAW

ROGER WORTHINGTON: A PLACE FOR PEACE AND CONTEMPLATION

The last resting place of the Baptist preacher, Roger Worthington

Roger Worthington is not buried in a churchyard nor in any other consecrated ground but in a field to the side of Holcombe Hey Fold Farm above Hawkshaw, which lies between Ramsbottom and Bolton.

Just past the Wagon and Horses public house you will see a small whitewashed cottage with a post box set into its wall. This used to be the post office. If you head up the hill from here, along Hawkshaw Lane for about a mile – it is possible to drive but the lane becomes very narrow – past the Boardmans cottages and go to the top of the hill then turn to the left, you will find the grave, situated in a small walled garden area near Lower Grainings Farm.

An engraved stone at the entrance asks that 'Visitors are requested to honour this sacred spot'. As you step over the low stone stile, you find yourself in a small garden that overlooks the valley beyond. This was a place where Roger Worthington liked to sit and contemplate in peace and solitude and it is the place in which he chose to be buried.

There are two gravestones lying side by side: the original one from the year of his death in 1709 and a newer one placed here in July 1935, when the site of the grave was dedicated as a place of public solitude. The newer gravestone is inscribed:

> *This stone commemorates the death and burial of Roger Worthington, a Baptist preacher who ministered in this neighbourhood for many years. The old tombstone (originally placed here in 1709) was renovated and this stone provided in July 1935. The following inscription appeared on the old tombstone:*

> 'Here lies the body of Roger Worthington who departed this life on the 9th day of July 1709 about the 50th year of his age.'

> *They that serve Christ in faith and love*
> *shall ever reign with him above.*

There appears to be a degree of myth and legend surrounding Roger Worthington. The legend suggests that he was born a Roman Catholic in around 1659 and that, after early contact with dissidents, he renounced his faith and became a Baptist preacher ministering to the isolated hamlets of Hawkshaw and Holcombe in the late 17th century. An entry in the Bury parish register identifies him as a Dipper – a reference to his supposed practice of baptising converts in a pool at the front of Holcombe Hey Fold Farm, where he lived in one of the cottages. It is said that he was disinherited by his parents for giving up his Roman Catholic faith and that is the reason he was buried in unconsecrated ground.

The story of Roger Worthington needs to be told within the wider context of what was happening in the country as a whole at that time. Following the death of Oliver Cromwell in 1658 and the unwillingness of the English army to back his son Richard as Protector, General George Monk marched to London and took control of Parliament and the monarchy was restored. Charles II was brought home from Holland and his pro-Royalist Parliament attempted to deal with religious persecution by passing an Act of Uniformity in 1662, which imposed the use of the Book of Common Prayer in religious services and insisted that clergy subscribe to the Anglican doctrine. Those who refused to obey this law became known as Nonconformists, or dissenters. Around 2,000 members of the clergy resigned their livings as a matter of principle and some Nonconformists went to prison because they were unwilling to give up their religious beliefs.

It was during these years that Roger Worthington was growing up. Records show that he originally came from Salford and a house that he owned there was registered in 1706 as a Dissenters' Meeting House. His will, written in 1707, describes him as a yeoman of Salford but, when he died in 1709, he is described as living at Holcombe Hey Fold Farm, which he owned. Research shows that he was married with two children. His widow Martha and daughter Mary were last heard of in 1720 in Nantwich, Cheshire, and his son John was a gentleman in Shrewsbury.

A booklet was written in 1909 by Revd W.T. Kershaw of Ramsbottom, the pastor of the church, to commemorate the bi-centenary of Roger Worthington's death. In it he comments on the obscure history of Roger Worthington but says that 'there is also sufficient reason in regarding him not only as a Nonconformist, but as a Baptist, and that in his day and long afterwards he was always known, not as a Baptist minister as some have styled him, but as a Baptist preacher – an unordained layman'.

Although Roger Worthington's will makes no allusions to his religious beliefs, it mentions 'a bargain' which he had made with a Robert Walker which he asks his widow to confirm. It is thought that this bargain was an agreement for his body to be buried in the field adjoining Holcombe Hey Fold Farm. This was not some eccentric whim on his part. As a Nonconformist, Roger Worthington would have had a horror of his funeral being conducted according to the rites of the Book of Common Prayer and so would not have wanted his body to be buried in the local churchyard by an Anglican priest. He was not the only person to protest in this way; in 1751 the Revd

Richard Ashworth of Cloughfold Baptist church was buried in his own garden according to his wishes.

In the booklet written 100 years ago by Revd Kershaw, I found a handwritten letter in which he asks for a subscription to offset the cost of producing his pamphlet which is 'an effort to rescue the name of a Nonconformist worthy from threatened oblivion and to perpetuate his memory'. He also bemoans the sorry state of Roger Worthington's grave and describes the gravestone as 'broken into several pieces, and one or two pieces are missing'. He pleads for public assistance to restore the grave.

I am not sure when Revd Kershaw died, but I hope he may have seen the restoration of the grave in 1935. I am also sure that he would be thrilled with the site as it is today, because a few years ago the gravesite was once again restored by local volunteers who cleared away decades of overgrowth after investigations revealed that the land was owned by Bury Council. The volunteers worked to clear weeds and prune bushes. A form and a picnic bench were added for visitors to sit and rest awhile in this peaceful place.

Roger Worthington chose a beautiful, tranquil place for his body to be buried and it is well worth the effort involved in finding and visiting the grave for the magnificent views from the top of the hill, and also to ponder on this country's present tolerance of all religious beliefs.

HEYSHAM

An ancient burial ground and rock-hewn graves

Heysham is a quaint little village on the southern coast of Morecambe Bay. I remember visiting it as a child when you could still buy nettle beer from a stall on the main street. The stall isn't there now but you can still sit on the brass beam scale and get weighed in public, if you are brave enough.

Most visitors make their way up Main Street, past St Patrick's Well and into St Peter's churchyard. The small, squat church is one of the oldest in Lancashire, dating from around the Norman Conquest. Inside, some of the pews are by windows that look out over the bay; you could probably draw more divine inspiration from that view than from a dozen boring sermons – and probably many worshippers over the years have watched the oystercatchers, curlew and redshank wading on the shoreline from here.

Outside, a stroll around the graveyard is fascinating if only to count the number of deaths by drowning – one of the graves with railings is of two teenage girls who were drowned on the incoming tide during the last century. The earliest marked graves, some dating from the 1700s, are mostly close to the church, with the flat gravestones usually being older than the upright stones. The lower graveyard, near the sea wall, dates from 1903 and most of the graves are quite plain giving the place an atmosphere of tranquillity and simple tribute to the dead.

The grave of two sisters drowned off the shore at Heysham

Inside the church there is a 'crusader's tomb' – a medieval sepulchral slab carved with a floriated cross and sword that may have once covered a grave. There is also a hog-back stone that was discovered in the churchyard but taken inside in 1961 to prevent further weather damage. It dates from the 10th century and it is thought that it could have come from the grave of a Viking chief. It is beautifully preserved and may show a story said to come from the pseudo-Gospel of Nicodemus telling how, on the death of Adam, Eve and Seth travelled to paradise to find a holy vessel in which was stored a drop of the Redeemer's blood. This may have been the origin of the legends of the Holy Grail. On the journey they fought evil spirits who tried to turn them back; one side of the stone shows this conflict, the other side shows their return in triumph.

To see even older graves you must climb the narrow stone steps to the cliff top, where the ruin of St Patrick's chapel dominates the windy headland. Legend tells that St Patrick was shipwrecked here but was lucky enough to stumble ashore and that he built this chapel as a thanksgiving. It seems more likely that it was built later, around AD 750, and may have been a small monastery, possibly constructed to honour the remains of the inhabitants of the graves.

There are eight rock graves in total: six to the west of the chapel and two to the south-east. They are empty now, or filled with water on rainy days. A base for a cross or headstone is cut by some and they are thought to be amongst the earliest examples of Christian burial in the country. Of course nobody knows for sure who was buried in them, though they probably were only for the privileged. To the south of the chapel is an ancient burial ground where 85 sets of bones were found during an archaeological excavation in the early 1970s.

The rock graves, which would have been covered by stone slabs, seem very small, though it has been suggested that this could be explained by the fact that they were ossuaries, where only the bones of the deceased where placed. If that is true then the small chapel could have been the place where bodies were left to decompose prior to burial.

St Patrick's Chapel is a Scheduled Ancient Monument and is now owned by the National Trust, along with the rock-hewn graves, the adjacent burial grounds and part of Heysham Head. It is a picturesque spot to visit and I often wonder who those people were who were laid to rest gazing out towards the Lake District hills.

The rock-hewn graves at Heysham

LANGHO

Brockhall Hospital graveyard: a grassy field with a sombre secret

The parish church of St Leonard at Langho was built in 1879, after a settlement grew up along the road and railway from Blackburn to Clitheroe. However, an older church, also called St Leonard's, can still be found near the original village of Old Langho about a mile away. This church was built in 1557 during the short reign of Queen Mary, sometimes known as Bloody Mary for her religious persecutions. It is one of very few churches built for Roman Catholic worship after the Reformation. Constructed soon after Henry VIII's dissolution of the monasteries,

The memorial to some of those who died in Brockhall Hospital

it is believed that the stones were taken from nearby Whalley Abbey.

The church is not now in use, though it is open to visitors most Sunday afternoons between 2 pm and 4 pm. The small, low structure has a simple roof and five square-headed windows. There is also a holy water stoop and a credence table on which the monks celebrated their communion mass.

There is a small graveyard surrounding the church, but adjacent to it is another graveyard. It can be reached from the road, down a short path that leads to a lychgate which marks the cemetery entrance. Here lie the remains of over 600 patients who died at the nearby Brockhall Hospital.

The hospital, originally called the Lancashire Inebriates Reformatory, was opened on 14th April 1904 by Sir John Hibbert, the Chairman of the

Lancashire Inebriates Acts Board. In his speech, he said it was his 'heart-felt wish that all inmates who might come within its walls would, by its means, be restored to happier and brighter lives'.

Brockhall was built on 326 acres of land that had been two farms, purchased from Mr Worsley Taylor for £17,000. The original building cost £67,000 and the estate was described as 'an extremely attractive one, a large proportion of it comprising an elevated plateau of grassland, surrounded on three sides by a belt of well-grown timber, while from the plateau there is a slope to some meadow and pastureland, which runs alongside the southerly bank of the River Ribble'.

An idyllic spot for an institution, the wards for men were named after trees or woodland, and the women's and children's wards after flowers. At its peak it was home to 2,500 patients and was known by several names: Brockhall Hospital for Mental Defectives (1915), Brockhall Hospital for the Mentally Subnormal (1959), Brockhall Hospital for Mentally Handicapped People (1974), and Brockhall Hospital for People with Learning Disabilities (1991).

At first, patients who died here and whose bodies were not taken to be buried by relatives, either because no relatives could be traced or because they chose to have the remains buried locally, were interred in the churchyard of St Leonard's. In the 1930s, because the churchyard was becoming full, it was decided that the hospital should have its own cemetery and a nearby field was allocated for this purpose, though later the churchyard was extended and the two graveyards became adjacent.

It was only in the late 1980s that the hospital authorities decided to stop using the cemetery for new burials. The hospital was closed in 1992 and the land was redeveloped for housing and is now known as Brockhall Village. However, the graveyard remains and Gerald Hitman, the property developer who owns the land, decided to mark the burial ground with a memorial at his own expense. It reads:

In an isolated institution located to the north east of this stone there lived from 1904 to 1992 a large number of people who were thought to be too strange, too difficult or too challenging to be cared for in their own communities. The institution in turn was called Lancashire Inebriates

Reformatory (1904) Brockhall Hospital for Mental Defectives (1915) Brockhall Hospital for the Mentally Subnormal (1959) Brockhall Hospital for Mentally Handicapped People (1974) and Brockhall Hospital for People with Learning Disabilities (1991). Although those who lived there carried heavier burdens than most they were part of our common family. Brockhall Hospital closed its doors in 1992 and the land on which it stood was acquired by Gerald Shimon Hitman of Newcastle upon Tyne who raised this stone as a memorial to those who ended their days in the hospital and are buried here. God full of compassion grant perfect rest beneath the shelter of your presence to these your children who have gone to their eternal home. Master of mercy, cover them in the shelter of your wings forever and bind their souls into the gathering of life. It is the Lord who is their heritage. May they be at peace in their place of rest.

The memorial lists many of the names of those buried although there are many more whose names are not known, including many who were cremated and whose ashes were buried near to the path.

Although a few of the graves are marked with headstones or small memorials most are unmarked and the remains lie hidden under what appears to be a grassy field. It is a tranquil and beautiful spot but one which holds a sombre secret.

LYTHAM

LIFEBOATS, BUSINESS AND FOOTBALL

The men of the Lytham and St Annes lifeboats

Near the main door of St Annes parish church there are two graves side by side. One is a large red sandstone memorial and the grave of five members of the St Annes lifeboat crew. Erected by public subscription, and recently restored, the memorial lists the names of Charles Tims age 43, Reuben Tims age 30, Thomas Bonneyage age 35, James H. Dobson age 28 and Thomas Parkinson age 28, who died in the attempted rescue of the crew of the *Mexico* on the night of the 9th December 1886. The memorial is also inscribed with words from the gospel of St John: 'Greater Love Hath No Man Than This. That A Man lay down His Life For His Friends.'

The *Mexico* was a large barque from Hamburg which was sailing from Liverpool to Guayaquil, Ecuador's largest city and main port. The ship sent out a distress signal south-west of Lytham. At around 10 pm the Lytham lifeboat, *Charles Biggs*, was launched in a moderate west-north-west gale, with a very heavy sea. At 11 pm that same night the lifeboat from Southport, the *Eliza Fernley* was also launched and managed to come within about 20 yards of the *Mexico*, which was breaking up, when a huge wave struck the lifeboat, tipping her upside down. Her crew were washed into the raging sea and were all drowned except for two survivors. At

The Laura Janet memorial

around 10.30 pm the St Annes boat, *Laura Janet*, had also set out, under sail, but she was quickly swept away. The boat from Lytham eventually managed to reach the *Mexico*, plucking the captain and crew from the sinking vessel and bringing them safely to shore. Coxswain Thomas Clarkson was awarded the RNLI's Silver Medal for the rescue. The crew then went back into the raging sea to try to save those on the St Annes boat. But they were too late. All the crew of the St Annes boat drowned. A total of 27 lifeboat men died at sea that night in what was possibly the worst RNLI disaster on record.

At St Cuthbert's church in Lytham there is a memorial to the crew of the *Laura Janet*, where other members of the drowned crew are buried: James Bonney age 21, Nicholas Parkinson age 22, Richard Fisher age 45, Oliver Hodson age 39, James Johnson age 45, John P. Wignall age 22 and William Johnson (coxswain) age 35. There is also mention of James Harrison, age 19, who is buried in Blackpool cemetery.

Charles Macara

The grave alongside the memorial at St Annes is that of Sir Charles Wright Macara. He was born in 1845 at Strathmiglo in Fifeshire and was the eldest son of Revd William Macara, who was a minister in the Free Church of Scotland. After being educated by his father and at school in Edinburgh he began, at the age of 16, to work for a firm in Glasgow, whose business took him on visits to Manchester where he subsequently worked as a representative of Cox Brothers of Dundee. In 1880 he became a partner in the firm of Henry Bannerman and Sons and acted as the managing director from 1884. In 1875 he married Marion, who was a granddaughter of one of the founders of the firm.

In 1884 he fought a strike by the Bannerman workers but became associated with the rights of both workers and employers. From 1894 until 1914 he was president of the Federation of Master Cotton Spinners' Associations and, in 1899, was instrumental in the formation of the Manchester Cotton Employers' Parliamentary Association. During the cotton strike of 1892–3 he resisted the workers' wage demands but also opposed employers' attempts to crush the union and, as chairman of the Manchester Master Cotton Spinners' Association, he was largely responsible for the Brooklands Agreement of 1893 which established new guidelines for negotiations during labour disputes within the cotton industry.

Charles Macara's grave at St Annes

From 1885 he spent his weekends at St Annes where he loved to sail. When donations to help the bereaved families of the *Mexico* disaster were received, including contributions from Queen Victoria, the German Emperor and the Port of Hamburg, he became chairman of the Relief Fund. Following this, he founded the Lifeboat Saturday Fund. The first fund-raising event was held in 1891, in Manchester, when 30,000 people attended and £5,500 was collected. The Fund spread to the rest of the country and became an annual event. Marion Macara helped set up the Ladies Auxiliary Committee which led later to the formation of the Ladies Lifeboat Guilds. Charles Macara revolutionised charity fundraising and his ideas still raise money for the Royal National Lifeboat Institution.

Charles Macara was created a baronet in 1911. He died at his home at Hale, Cheshire, on 2nd January 1929, but was buried at St Annes.

Harry Catterick

Another interesting grave to be found at St Annes parish church, on the left-hand side of the path that leads to the south from the lifeboat memorial, is that of Harry Catterick. He was manager of Everton Football Club during one of its most successful periods, from 1961 to 1973. Despite his reputation of being a strict disciplinarian, he commanded the respect of his players and everyone who met him.

The grave of Harry Catterick

Under his guidance Everton won the Football League Championship in the 1962/63 season, went on to win the FA Cup in 1966 and only narrowly missed winning again in 1968. The team won the Championship again in 1969/70, but the seventies brought a downturn in their fortunes. Harry Catterick had a heart attack in 1972 and in 1973 he stepped down as manager to take on a non-executive role.

Shortly after watching Everton beat Ipswich Town in the FA Cup quarter-final at Goodison Park he collapsed and died on 9th March 1985.

MIDDLETON

SAMUEL BAMFORD: POET, WEAVER AND ACTIVIST

Samuel Bamford is buried in the graveyard of Middleton parish church, where a memorial obelisk can be found to the side of the main path as it slopes down towards the main road.

Samuel Bamford is remembered in the *Oxford Dictionary of National Biography* as a poet and a weaver, but it is for his efforts towards Parliamentary reform and universal suffrage, as well as his role in the Peterloo Massacre of 1819, that many remember him.

He was born at Middleton on 28th February 1788, but his parents, who were radical followers of John Wesley, later moved to Manchester where Samuel attended the Free Grammar School. Soon afterwards two of his brothers died of smallpox and his mother died of fever.

The imposing memorial to Samuel Bamford

His father later re-married and Samuel returned to Middleton to live with an uncle, where he continued to educate himself, as well as learning to weave. At the age of nineteen he walked to South Shields to work as a sailor on a coal ship but, being unhappy with that experience, he left the ship at London and walked home, narrowly escaping being press-ganged on the way.

After his own marriage in 1812 he and his wife set themselves up as handloom weavers. He continued to educate himself, enjoying the work of Milton, Shakespeare and Robert Burns, as well as books by radicals such as Tom Paine and William Cobbett.

As well as reading widely, Samuel loved to write. His poetry resonated with his fellow workers in Lancashire as he wrote about their difficult lives. Elizabeth Gaskell quotes from one of his poems that begins 'God help the poor' in her novel *Mary Barton*.

It was at this time that the government had introduced the Corn Laws. These laws were introduced to safeguard the economy from cheap imported corn and stated that corn could not be imported until home-grown corn had reached a certain price. The result was that corn became so expensive that the price of bread rose beyond the reach of the poor and many people began to starve.

Samuel Bamford became interested in Parliamentary reforms that would give the poor a voice in the running of the country rather than being at the mercy of the aristocracy. He was interested in the campaign of social reformer John Cartwright and, in 1816, Samuel formed the Middleton branch of the Hampden Club, where he joined in the call for universal suffrage, annual elections, secret ballots, equal electoral districts and the abolition of the so-called 'rotten boroughs' where constituencies that had declined in size, sometimes to only a handful of dwellings, were still returning a Member of Parliament who could easily bribe or bully their way to victory.

When the authorities heard about Samuel Bamford's activities he was arrested for high treason and imprisoned, but was later acquitted owing to insufficient evidence.

On 16th August 1819 Samuel Bamford headed a group of people from Middleton who went to a rally in Manchester to hear Henry Hunt and other radicals speak. Protesters from surrounding towns and villages assembled at St Peter's Field in Manchester, near where the Free Trade Hall was later built, with music and banners proclaiming 'No Corn Laws', 'Annual Parliaments', 'Universal Suffrage' and 'Vote By Ballot'.

His own account of what happened that day – the Peterloo Massacre – is probably the best source of historical evidence. Samuel Bamford describes how, as the meeting waited for Hunt to speak, cavalry, summoned by local magistrate William Hulton to quell a potential riot, rode up brandishing their sabres above their heads and spurring their horses into the crowd:

'Stand fast!' I said, 'they are riding upon us, stand fast.' And there was a general cry in our quarter of 'Stand fast!' The cavalry were in confusion; they could not, with all the weight of man and horse, penetrate that compact mass of human beings; their sabres were plied to hew a way through naked held-up hands, and defenceless heads; and then chopped limbs, and wound-gaping skulls were seen; and groans and cries were mingled with the din of that horrid confusion.

He goes on to describe the slaughter of men, women and children that resulted, just ten minutes later, in the field being deserted except for the dead and injured and: '*a torn and gashed banner or two drooping; whilst over the whole field were strewed caps, bonnets, hats, shawls, and shoes, and other parts of male and female dress, trampled, torn, and bloody.*' Eleven people were killed and over 500 were injured, many of them women, who were trampled by the horses.

The government supported the action of the army, and Samuel Bamford and several other men were arrested and charged with 'assembling with unlawful banners at an unlawful meeting for the purpose of inciting discontent'. He was sentenced to one year's imprisonment in Lincoln Prison, after which he records how he walked home to Middleton and ceased to be active in the campaign for Parliamentary reform.

'*We entered Middleton*', he says, '*in the afternoon, and were met in the streets by our dear child, who came running, wild with delight, to our arms. We soon made ourselves comfortable in our own humble dwelling; the fire was lighted, the hearth was clean swept, friends came to welcome us, and we were once more at home!*'

He returned to his handloom weaving, but the increasing competition from local factories meant that he struggled to earn enough to live on and he tried to supplement his income by selling his poetry.

In 1826 he became a correspondent of a London morning newspaper and, around 1851, obtained a fairly well paid job as a messenger in Somerset House. But he pined for Lancashire and after a few years returned home and took up his old trade as a weaver. He died on 13th April 1872 at Harpurhey, at the age of 84.

The Stanley effigies at Ormskirk

ORMSKIRK

THE EARLS OF DERBY AND THEIR WIVES

Thomas Stanley: 1st Earl of Derby and his two wives

In the Derby chapel of the parish church at Ormskirk you will find a pair of effigies on either side of the altar. Sometimes known locally as the king and queens of Man (as the Isle of Man was amongst the lands owned by the Stanley family), the carvings represent Thomas Stanley, 1st Earl of Derby and his two wives.

It is almost certain that the body of Thomas Stanley now resides in the family vault here, although his first wife, Eleanor Neville, and their eldest son, Lord George Strange, are buried at St James, Garlickhithe, in London. Eleanor Neville was the daughter of Richard Neville, Earl of Salisbury, and sister of Richard Neville, Earl of Warwick, sometimes known as the 'kingmaker' for his role in the Wars of the Roses.

LANCASHIRE Who Lies Beneath?

Thomas Stanley's second wife, Margaret Beaufort, was the mother of Henry Tudor by her first husband Edmund Tudor, Earl of Richmond, who was a half-brother to Henry VI. Edmund Tudor, a Lancastrian supporter, died during the Wars of the Roses and Margaret, aged thirteen, gave birth to Henry whom she idolised and whom she later helped to claim the throne as Henry VII. Her second marriage was to Sir Henry Stafford and, after being widowed for a second time, she married Thomas Stanley. Although her effigy is portrayed here, she is actually buried in Westminster Abbey, as befits the mother of a king. However, it is the ambiguous loyalties of her and Thomas Stanley during the reign of Richard III that make the most interesting part of the story.

Thomas Stanley first crossed swords with Richard when, as Duke of Gloucester, he was given land in Lancashire (the honour of Clitheroe) by his brother King Edward IV. The Harrington family of Hornby Castle had supported Richard's father, Richard Duke of York, at the battle of Wakefield. Sir Thomas Harrington was killed in the fighting and his eldest son, John, died of his wounds the next day, leaving the Hornby estate to his two infant daughters, Anne and Elizabeth. Despite a claim to the lands by John's younger brothers, James and Robert Harrington, the king ruled that the girls should inherit. They were eventually given into the guardianship of Lord Stanley, who quickly arranged for Anne to be married to his second son, Edward, and Elizabeth to another Stanley relative, John.

However, Richard decided that the girls' uncles had a better claim and although he was eventually overruled by a court of law, his interference had antagonised Thomas Stanley. Although the two of them gave the appearance of supporting one another in later years, there seems to have been an undercurrent of mistrust on both sides and Thomas Stanley appears to have been a man who always put his own interests first.

When Richard came to the throne as Richard III, Thomas Stanley, who was a powerful landowner in the north, appeared to back Richard as king. He carried the mace at Richard's coronation and his wife, Margaret Beaufort, carried the queen's train. When it was discovered that Margaret Beaufort had been plotting against the king and backing a rebellion that would place her own son Henry Tudor on the throne, Richard III only punished her by giving her lands to her husband and placing her under her husband's control.

Richard continued to keep Thomas Stanley within his close circle of friends and advisors, but whether this was because he trusted him or because he wanted to keep an eye on him is debatable. Secretly the Stanleys were both backing Henry Tudor. The king must have suspected his motives because when Thomas Stanley stayed too long in Lancashire the king ordered him to return or send his son, Lord Strange, in his place to ensure his loyalty; though when the king warned that he would execute Lord Strange unless Stanley swore to support him in battle, Stanley is said to have replied that he had other sons.

When Henry Tudor invaded England, King Richard expected Thomas and his brother William to fight with him against the rebels. The brothers gathered their armies and marched towards the site of the battle, near Leicester, but did not commit themselves one way or the other as the armies took their places. In fact, Thomas Stanley took no part at all in the battle of Bosworth and it was only when his brother William intervened on the Lancastrian side that Richard III was beaten and killed.

Thomas Stanley was rewarded with lands that had been seized from Lancashire families who had supported the Yorkists and he was created Earl of Derby. He officiated at the coronation of Henry VII and was later godfather to Arthur, the first-born son of the king and his queen, Elizabeth of York.

Thomas Stanley died at Lathom on 29th July 1504 and was buried with his ancestors at Burscough Priory. In his will Thomas Stanley recorded that he wanted his 'body to be buryed in the middest of the chapell in the North Ile of the Church of the Priory of Burscough' and in his will he also names the position to be occupied by the effigies of himself and his wives that he 'caused to be made'.

His body did not stay long in his desired resting place though. Ironically, when Henry VIII, the son of the king Stanley had helped to the throne, came to power he ordered the dissolution of the monasteries and Burscough Priory was destroyed. After the dissolution, the bones of family members were recovered and taken to the Derby Chapel at St Peter and St Paul in Ormskirk, which had been built by Edward Stanley, 3rd Earl of Derby. The effigies were also removed and taken to Ormskirk where, although worn and damaged, they can still be seen.

James Stanley, 7th Earl of Derby

Also buried in this vault is James Stanley, the 7th Earl, who was beheaded at Bolton in 1651. He has two coffins – one for his body and one for his head. James Stanley had remained a staunch supporter of Charles I during the Civil War. When he received news that the Scots were planning to invade Lancashire via the Isle of Man, which was still part of the Stanley estates, he left his home, Lathom House, in the care of his French-born wife and sailed to the island to prevent any landing by the Scots.

His wife, the Countess of Derby, Charlotte de Tremouille, daughter of a high-ranking French nobleman, had no intention of giving up her home without a fight. Despite requests to leave quietly, she refused, and eventually the Parliamentarians laid siege to the house. When Alexander Rigby from Preston, who had a personal grudge against Lord Derby, became a Colonel in the Parliamentary army he was determined to take Lathom House. He brought a mortar gun from London which he mounted on earthworks outside the walls of the house. Lady Derby knew she was in danger and that the only way to save herself was to stop Rigby using his mortar gun to bombard the house with the nail bombs he had recently acquired. So at four o'clock the following morning a party of men from the house came out of a gate, drove away the soldiers guarding the mortar gun and having tied ropes around it they dragged it inside the house walls.

Rigby sent for reinforcements but help was at hand for Lady Derby. Her relative, Prince Rupert, met up with Lord Derby who had returned from the Isle of Man. Together they entered Lancashire by Stockport Bridge on 25th May with an army of 10,000 men and, afraid of being surrounded, Rigby retreated.

Rigby believed that the army would march to York via either Blackburn or Lancaster so he retreated to Bolton to keep out of their way but, scarcely had he entered the town than he saw Prince Rupert's army coming over the moors at Deane. The battle between the Royalists and Parliamentarians became known as the Bolton Massacre. That same night Lord Derby and Prince Rupert entered Lathom in triumph and, of the 3,000 men led by Colonel Rigby, 1,500 were left dead and 700 taken prisoner.

After Cromwell's victory, James Stanley was hunted down and captured in Cheshire. Following a three-day trial, he was taken to Bolton, where he spent his last hours at Ye Olde Man and Scythe public house, before being beheaded in Churchgate on 15th October 1651.

ORRELL

John T. Alker: 'killed by electricity'

John T. Alker was not famous in life but his death was a tragedy. His tall granite memorial in the churchyard of St James' Roman Catholic church in Orrell, near Wigan, reads:

> *Sacred Heart of Jesus have Mercy on the Soul of*
> *John T. Alker of Winstanley.*
> *Killed by electricity – June 24th 1898. Aged 21 years.*

Well, an epitaph like that is obviously designed to provoke an interest. Had John T. Alker been struck by lightning? Or was his death altogether more sinister?

John was the younger son of a well-known farming family in the Winstanley district and was training as a mining student with J. and R. Stone at Park Collieries, Garswood, Ashton-in-Makerfield, which was about four miles from his home.

On the morning of Friday, 24th June 1898, he went down into the colliery's Number One Pit along with mining surveyor Frederick McGill, and colliery firemen John Cunliffe and Joseph Smalls. They were there to carry out an inspection of the mine where underground electrical lighting had been installed two days before.

They arrived at the 'pit bottom' just before 10.45 am and, to allow their eyes to adjust to the brightness of the new lighting, they stepped into the underlooker's cabin, which contained the control panel for both the lighting and the electrical pumping systems.

About half an hour later McGill, Cunliffe and Smalls left the cabin and began to walk along the roadway. When they realised that John Alker was not with them, they looked back and saw his head and shoulders hanging out of the doorway of the cabin, with his face contorted and obviously in severe pain. McGill ran back and saw that John was holding one of the switches on the electrical control panel. He shouted to Cunliffe and Smalls that Alker was 'stuck fast with the electricity'. The other two men ran back as Cunliffe turned off the current at the main switch. But they were too late. The lifeless body of the young man collapsed into the arms of Joseph Smalls.

They hurriedly took the body to the surface and called a doctor, but he pronounced John Alker dead and the police were summoned. PC Grantham of Ashton-in-Makerfield attended the scene. In line with accepted legal procedures, the deceased should have been taken to the nearest public house and a coroner's jury called to view the body so that arrangements could be made for an inquest at a later date at those premises. But by this time John Alker's father, Robert Alker, had been informed and he came and demanded that his son's body should be taken home without delay. PC Grantham warned him that the body could not be removed without the coroner's consent but Robert Alker was insistent and was supported by the colliery manager, Mr Hilton, who provided a horse-drawn brake for the body to be taken back to Winstanley.

Although it was understandable that Robert Alker wished to take his son's body home, it did lead to complications. When the coroner for south-west Lancashire, Mr Samuel Brighouse, opened the inquest three days later, on 27th June 1898 at the Railway Hotel, Orrell, he was not a happy man.

The inquest began with Robert Alker junior representing his father, Robert, who was unfit to attend. He testified that he had last seen his younger brother at about 8 am on the morning that he died when he appeared in good health, and that he had been present when the deceased was brought home some few hours later. It was at this point that the coroner, Mr Brighouse, called PC Grantham and said:

'I want some explanation as to how it came about that the deceased's body has been removed out of the township of Ashton into the township of Orrell without my consent. I have been told that the deceased's father insisted on removing the body to Orrell. I have been informed that the colliery manager also approved of the body being removed. What is the result? The body was removed into the township of Orrell, and the gentlemen of that township have to inquire into the cause of death, when the jury of Ashton ought to have done so. All this inconvenience has been caused by an illegal and irregular action. They might as well have moved the body to London. I quite appreciate and sympathise with the parents wishing the body to be removed home, I would have done so as well, but certain formalities have to be gone through before that can be done, and they could have removed the deceased the same day, if they had communicated with me.'

The poor police constable could only reply that he had warned Mr Alker that his actions were illegal. The coroner went on to tell them that if the same thing ever happened again he would have the body sent back. Thus, having aired his views and stamped his authority on the proceedings, he continued with the inquest.

John T. Alker's grave

Frederick McGill gave evidence that he had seen John Alker leaning out of the cabin in obvious pain and that, when he went into the cabin, he saw the deceased's hand holding a switch on the electrical control panel, although the deceased had no reason to operate the switchboard.

John Cunliffe told how he had switched off the current when he saw the deceased's hand on the switch and also explained that whilst the deceased was holding the insulated switch handle between his forefinger and thumb, his remaining three fingers were resting on the 'live' metalwork beneath the handle and this is what had caused the shock.

Mr Matthews, a Mines Inspector, was then called and he said that he was of the opinion that youthful curiosity had brought about John Alker's death and the fact that he was looking out of the door of the cabin would seem to suggest that he was looking to see if the switch he was holding operated the lighting system. This theory was accepted.

Though it seems strange that the switchboard was so dangerous to the touch, Mr Allen, representing the company that was responsible for the electrical installation, said that there were similar switchboards all over the country, and that the power of the current was not normally enough to kill a healthy man. He said that he knew of many colliery workers who had suffered shocks with no ill effects and that as John Alker had recently suffered from a bout of typhoid fever, it could have been this that had weakened him enough for the shock to kill him.

Other technical evidence followed but the coroner decided not to order a post-mortem examination of the body and told the jury that their verdict seemed to be only a formality. He told them, 'You are entitled to take into consideration the circumstances under which he received the shock, and if you have a suggestion which would tend to preserve life in the future, you will be entitled to add that suggestion.'

The returned verdict was that John T. Alker had died as the result of an electric shock received from the switchboard in the mine. The jury recommended that, in future, switchboards should be operated by one authorised person and that 'live' components should be boxed in and the handles better insulated. They also offered a vote of sympathy to the relatives of the deceased. But what I find difficult to put out of my mind is the image of his parents insisting that the words 'killed by electricity' should be inscribed on his grave. Poor John, the electricity had been installed in the mine as a safety measure, but his natural curiosity and interest in it was the death of him.

PENDLE AND GISBURN

WITCHES' GRAVES

Alice Nutter

There is a grave near the south wall of the church at Newchurch in Pendle that has earned the reputation as being that of a witch. As well as a skull and crossbones, it has engraved on it the names of various members of a family by the name of Nutter and the area is well known for its connections with the Lancashire witches, one of whom was Alice Nutter.

The mysterious grave at Newchurch

Alice Nutter lived nearby at Roughlee Hall. She was brought to trial at Lancaster on 19th August 1612 before Sir Edward Bromley, one of James I's Justices of Assize at Lancaster. Judge Altham was also present and the judges were assisted by Lord Gerard and Sir Richard Hoghton. The Prosecutor was a former High Sheriff of Lancashire, Roger Nowell of Read Hall, near Burnley. He had gathered the evidence and sent the accused for trial. The accused, however, were not allowed to have anyone to plead their case or to call witnesses to speak on their behalf.

In his book *The Wonderfull Discoverie of Witches in the Countie of Lancaster,* Thomas Potts, who was a clerk to the court, says about Alice Nutter: 'For it is certain she was a rich woman; had a great estate, and children of good hope: in the common opinion of the world, of good temper, free from envy or malice.'

The first charge brought against her was that she had helped to bewitch to death a man called Mitton because he had refused to give Old Demdike a penny. The evidence against her was given by James Device, the grandson of Old Demdike. He said that his grandmother, Old Demdike, his mother, Elizabeth Device, and Alice Nutter, wife of Richard Nutter of the Rough-Lee, had killed one Henry Mitton, also of the Rough-Lee, by witchcraft.

The second charge was that she was present at Malkin Tower on 10th April 1612 – Good Friday. This charge was brought on evidence from both Elizabeth Device and her son James Device. One reason for this meeting, it was claimed, was to plan to kill the gaoler at Lancaster and to blow up the castle before the next Assizes so that the prisoners, including Old Demdike, her sister Anne Chattox and her daughter Anne Redfearne, who were already being held on charges of witchcraft, could escape. James Device also stated that the witches left the house in their own forms but, as soon as they were outside, changed into horses or foals.

The next evidence read to the court against Alice Nutter had been given by Jennet Device, the nine-year-old sister of James. But Potts records that '... his Lordship being very suspicious of the accusation of this young wench, Jennet Device, commanded one to take her away into the Upper Hall, intending in the meantime to make Trial of her Evidence.' He had some other women brought in and instructed them to stand amongst the prisoners before bringing Jennet back. Potts records that 'He took great pains to examine her of every particular point. What women were at Malkin Tower upon Good Friday? How she knew them? What were the names of any of them? And how she knew them to be such as she named?'

Then he asked her to identify the women who had been at Malkin Tower. The girl went straight to Alice Nutter and took her hand and told the judge where she had sat and what she had said at the 'great assembly of the witches'. The judge then asked her about another woman but Jennet told him she did not know her or recognise her. It was concluded that there was no false or forged accusation against Alice Nutter and that she was guilty. She was hanged at Lancaster, though Potts records that she remained impenitent and that her refusal to confess her sins before she died 'was a very fearful thing to all that were present, who knew she was guilty'.

There is no record of what happened to the bodies of the Lancashire witches, though the grave at Newchurch probably does not contain the body of Alice Nutter. It is doubtful that the body of an executed witch would be buried in consecrated ground; usually the bodies were burned, put into a mass grave or sent for medical research. But it does act as a reminder of the death of a woman who was convicted on the flimsiest of evidence and who, some say, was a victim of a conspiracy within her own family.

Jennet Preston

In the churchyard of St Mary's at Gisburn, you will find a small, iron headstone. The image carved on it looks rather like a witch's cauldron and it is said to mark the grave of Jennet Preston.

Jennet Preston lived near Westby Hall, a moated manor house owned by Thomas Lister, the main landowner in Gisburn. Although she is probably the Jennet Balderstone who married William Preston at St Mary's church in the village on 10th May 1587, she appears to have had a special relationship with the lord of the manor and Thomas Potts records that she 'had access to his house, kind respect and entertainment; nothing denied her that she stood in need of'.

Thomas Lister died in 1608 at the age of 38 at around the time when his son, also Thomas Lister, was married to Jane Heaber of Marton, daughter of Thomas Heaber.

Soon afterwards things on the estate appeared to go wrong. The new master was only 17 years old and seems to have lost many of his goods and cattle, which he later blamed on Jennet's witchcraft. He had her brought before Sir Edward Bromley at the Lent Assizes at York in 1612 on a charge of having murdered, by witchcraft, a child of a family named Dodgeson. But there must have been very little evidence as she was acquitted of the charge.

The witch's grave at Gisburn

Four days later, on Good Friday, 10th April 1612 she was allegedly one of the women present at Malkin Tower. But as Gisburn was, at that time in the county of Yorkshire, Jennet Preston is not always included when reference is made to the Lancashire witches. Evidence gathered against the Lancashire witches said that Jennet Preston had joined them on Good Friday to ask for help in murdering Thomas Lister, who had been her accuser at York. When Lister discovered this, he had her sent to the July Assizes in York, where she was now accused of the murder of his father, Thomas Lister senior, four years earlier. The prosecuting magistrate was Thomas Heaber of Marton, Thomas Lister's father-in-law.

Although she pleaded not guilty, there was, supposedly, the most damning evidence given against her. This 'evidence' was that when she was taken to see Thomas Lister's body after his death she had touched the corpse and it had bled fresh blood. In those days it was a widely held belief that a corpse would bleed afresh in the presence of its murderer. Witnesses at this trial also swore on oath that Thomas Lister on his death bed had 'cried out unto them that stood about him that Jennet Preston was in the house, look where she is, take hold on her, for God's sake shut the doors and take her, so she cannot escape away'. And although from this it could be assumed that he had died at home, according to parish registers he died at Bracewell during the same week in February that his son was married there to Jane Heaber.

Other evidence against her was given: 'That when Master Lister lay upon his death-bed he cried out in great extremity, "Jennet Preston lies heavy upon me, Preston's wife lies heavy upon me; help me, help me" and so departed, crying out against her.' But was he crying against her? Why was her name on his lips as he died? Because he thought she had bewitched him to death? Or was there another reason? In the book *The Lancashire Witches: Histories and Stories* edited by Robert Poole, Jonathan Lumby suggests that Jennet Preston had been Thomas Lister's mistress.

Whatever the truth, Thomas Lister junior seems to have been very keen to be rid of her for one reason or another. With the help of his father-in-law, she was convicted as a witch on 27th July 1612 and sentenced to death by hanging. It isn't proven that the churchyard at Gisburn does actually contain her body. The iron headstone carries no name and may have simply been placed there in her memory. If it is not a memorial to Jennet Preston, then what the engraving represents remains a mystery.

QUERNMORE

THE QUERNMORE BURIAL

Many motorists driving through the picturesque Trough of Bowland stop at the Jubilee Tower to climb up and look at the panoramic vista of Morecambe Bay in the distance and even, on a clear day, the Isle of Man.

When the car park was being made in 1973, an ancient burial was found. On Saturday, 17th March, local man James Marshall was walking his dog when he noticed an object that he thought looked like a canoe which had been uncovered. Thinking that it might be of some archaeological interest, he quickly contacted the staff of the Lancaster City Museum to come and take a closer look.

A search of the surrounding area revealed more fragments of timber and two large pieces of woollen cloth. The items were all preserved by wrapping them in damp newspaper and polythene sheeting before they were taken to the museum for further analysis.

At Lancaster the fragments of timber were assembled like a jigsaw and it was discovered that they formed a second canoe-shaped object, which had apparently been intact until it was broken by the mechanical digger excavating the land.

The two pieces of woollen cloth were opened out in a specially constructed trough of water to prevent the fibres being damaged as the fragile textile was handled. They were found to have originally been one rectangle, though one corner had been cut off. But the most exciting discovery was a mass of reddish hair at the top corner, in the centre of the cloth some fingernails and in the detached portion some toenails. It was now apparent that these pieces of wood were not canoes at all but two pieces of an oak coffin, made from a single tree trunk, that would originally have been pegged together and that the woollen cloth was a burial shroud.

Most of the body had long since decomposed in the acidic conditions of the moorland peat, but the hair and nails, being composed of the protein keratin, were more resistant to decay and so these remained when all other traces of the body had disappeared.

Samples of the hair were sent to the police forensic unit at Chorley, where

LANCASHIRE Who Lies Beneath?

The memorial that commemorates the discovery of an ancient burial site

it was found that the reddish colour was not original but was because of staining from the peat soil and the oak of the coffin. The brownish shroud, which is the largest piece of woollen fabric from that era to be found in England, had also been affected and its original colour and pattern were no longer visible.

Radiocarbon dating of the timber resulted in a 90% chance that it was from between AD 424 and AD 864 during the Dark Ages when Anglo-Saxons, Celts or possibly Norse people would have lived in the area.

Who was buried is still a mystery, though the place of burial and the care taken over the coffin and the shroud suggest that it was someone important. This place, high on the moors overlooking the coast, would have been as special to those people who stood there over 1,000 years ago, as it is to visitors now. It may even have been a sacred place where the spirit of the deceased could overlook their land, or a place from which the spirit of the deceased could move on to another world. But whoever was buried there so carefully has now gained some degree of an afterlife as what remains of the burial is now displayed at the Lancaster City Museum.

RIBCHESTER

PLAGUE AND ACCIDENT

The Black Death

In the early 1340s, rumours began to circulate in English villages that a great pestilence had seized countries in the east, preceded by earthquakes and volcanic eruptions. This fast-spreading and virulent disease became better known as the Black Death. Around half the world's population died in the pandemic. Europe lost one-third of its population between 1347 and 1350, and England lost 70% of its population, which declined from seven million before the plague, to two million in 1400.

The Black Death spread westwards to Greece and through the Mediterranean into Italy and France. Many people believed that this plague had been sent by God to punish the infidel. Jews, lepers and foreigners were all blamed for the illness and many were murdered. Some believed that it would not harm Christians, but those who had seen its effects began to realise that nothing would stop it.

Prayer, penitence and medieval medicine all proved ineffective and in the village of Ribchester it is thought that up to 300 bodies, possibly around half the population, were buried at St Wilfrid's church in a mass grave under the north chapel that is now known as the Dutton Choir. No one was spared, not even monks and priests. The situation became so dire that physicians and lay people were given permission to hear the confessions of the dying, though the sick were often abandoned out of fear.

Research has pointed to the plague being caused by a viral infection, though it could be true that the deaths occurred from a range of diseases. The Black Death may have been a general term for three types of plague that were rife at this time and which recurred in later years, the best known being the Great Plague. There was bubonic plague, spread by flea bites, where four out of five victims died within eight days; pneumonic plague, an illness of the lungs which caused sufferers to cough up blood and which killed 90% of its victims; and septicaemic plague, or blood poisoning, with a mortality rate close to 100%.

It was not the Black Death in isolation that caused problems. A very

St Wilfrid's church where a mass grave was found

wet summer had prevented the corn from ripening and many villages were affected by flooding. Ribchester, with its proximity to the River Ribble, could have been one of these. Food prices soared and, coupled with growth in population, resulted in widespread famine and vulnerability to disease.

The Black Death changed the country forever and had particular ramifications for Lancashire. So many peasants died that the feudal system fell apart because there were not enough people to work the land for the local lord of the manor. The few who were left found that the laws of supply and demand allowed them to ask for more money in return for their labour; and the landowners realised that they could make more money by grazing sheep on their fields than by paying people to farm it. The sheep farming led to the woollen industry, which gave way to the cotton industry in Lancashire where the spinning and weaving skills already existed. In turn, this led to mills and towns and the movement of population to urban areas. Even the village of Ribchester had cotton mills at one time. It is sad to think that all those people who died and are buried in the churchyard resulted, in a roundabout way, in the prosperity of the county in the 19th and 20th centuries.

Thomas Greenwood

Another interesting grave just to the left of the church path as you approach the door is that of Thomas Greenwood. If you pause to read the slightly faded inscription you will discover that:

> Here lie thy body of Tho. Greenwood who died May 14 AD 1776 in y 52nd year of his age. Honest Industrious seeming still content. Nor did repine at what he underwent. His transient life was with hard labour filled. And working in a marlpit was killed.

Marle is a clay deposit which is rich in calcium carbonate. These sub soils were dug from deep pits by local farmers and ploughed into lighter soils in a process known as marling to improve their texture and fertility. Marling was part of the local way of life and a gang of five or six men would have taken around a fortnight to dig out enough marle to treat the fields. Once the pits had been dug, they gradually filled with water and many small ponds still around today were originally marl pits.

Falling into these deep pits seems to have been not unusual. Even Chaucer in his *Miller's Tale* tells of a man who fell into a marle pit. And there is a death recorded in the burial register at St Anne's in Turton, of a son of Will and Jane Loe whose name is given as Ed. He also died in a marle pit and was buried at Bolton on 12th June 1727.

Thomas Greenwood's grave at St Wilfrid's

ROCHDALE

A DIALECT POET AND A QUAKER PARLIAMENTARIAN

John Collier – also known as Tim Bobbin

John Collier has been described as the Robert Burns of Lancashire. Under his pen-name Tim Bobbin, he was the first author to write in the Lancashire dialect. His grave can be found in the churchyard of St Chad's, at Rochdale, where he is buried with his wife, Mary. The epitaph on the grave reads:

> *Here lies John with his Mary*
> *cheek by jowl they never vary;*
> *No wonder they do so agree,*
> *John wants no punch and Moll no tea.*

As John Collier was a dialect poet, some people believe that this verse may have been written by him. Some say he composed it ten minutes before he died, though it is also ascribed to his son.

John Collier's father was a curate and schoolmaster at a time when many

The grave of John Collier, alias Tim Bobbin

ROCHDALE

clerical 'livings' or 'benefices' were held by someone who enjoyed the income whilst paying a curate a miserly sum of money to do all the work. The Collier family were consequently very poor and John was the third son, born into a family of nine children. In later writing he describes being: '… one of nine children of a poor curate in Lancashire, whose stipend never amounted to thirty pounds a year, and consequently the family must feel the iron teeth of penury with a witness'. He also records that he lived on 'water porridge, buttermilk and jannock [oaten bread], till he was between 13 and 14 years of age, when Providence began to smile on him on his advancement to a pair of Dutch looms'.

Although his father had hoped that he would join the Church, their poverty made that impossible and instead John Collier was apprenticed to a Dutch born weaver named Johnson in May 1722.

At the age of 17 he made use of the education his father had given him and left the weaving trade to become a travelling schoolmaster, although the pay was very poor. He held daytime and evening classes in Bury, Middleton, Oldham and Rochdale and, as he travelled around, he began to make notes about the ways in which language and dialect was used in different towns and villages.

He later accepted the position of assistant master at a free school at Milnrow, near Rochdale, for a salary of ten pounds a year. He writes, 'I by divine Providence, vailing my skullcap to the mitres, in November 1727, commenced schoolmaster at Milnrow.' This 'vailing my skullcap to the mitres' referred to his gaining a licence from the Bishop, which he eventually received after teaching for 12 years as an assistant master and three years as the master after succeeding Mr Pearson, who had become ill with gout.

It was around this time that he began to write prose and verse under the pen-name of Tim Bobbin, as well as developing his talent for sketching portraits and caricatures.

On 1st April 1744 he married a girl from Yorkshire, Mary Clay, who had come to visit her aunt, Mrs Butterworth, at Milnrow. He was 35 years old and his bride was 21. They lived in a house near the school with a garden that overlooked the river. John reputedly spent much of his time there with his books and his flute while his students came from the school next door to have their work marked although it seems that this leisurely approach to life, along with the drinking and feasting at various inns in the vicinity, was prompted by the £300 that his wife brought to the marriage. However, soon the money was all gone and John Collier was forced to find a way of earning some more.

He began painting altarpieces for country churches and signboards for inns and later he toured around the inns selling caricatures to commercial travellers. He also wrote satires in both prose and verse and two years after his marriage he published *A View of the Lancashire Dialect* also known as the story of *Tummas and Meary*, which is a comic dialogue between two characters – Thomas and Mary. Written in Lancashire dialect, with a glossary of the Lancashire words and phrases he had collected over the years, it made Tim Bobbin a household name throughout the county even if didn't make his fortune.

He wrote prolifically and Chetham's library in Manchester holds one of the largest collections of material by and about Tim Bobbin, including many of his original manuscripts that demonstrate his interest in the Scots language, as well as his awareness of local affairs and current events.

He was still forced to earn a living, however, and five years after the publication of his book he was offered the well-paid post of head clerk by a Mr Hill of Halifax. He moved his wife and family to Yorkshire but sitting at a desk was anathema to him and, although he was receiving a house rent free and double the salary of that as a teacher, he persuaded Mr Hill to cancel their agreement and he returned to the house and school in Milnrow where his old job was still vacant. Here he continued to supplement his income by painting and writing and, although he seems to have been very fond of his drink, his wife Mary stood by him and they had six children. He died in July 1786 at the age of 77 just a few weeks after the death of Mary. They are both buried in the same grave, cheek by jowl.

John Bright

John Bright has both a grave and a statue in his memory at Rochdale. His grave is in the Society of Friends' Rochdale burial ground in Ball Street Gardens. Presently somewhat overgrown by grass, it is fashioned from white marble and merely records that: '*John Bright died March 27, 1889. Age, 77 years*'.

His bronze statue, in contrast, which can be found in Broadfield Park, is inscribed on all four sides and records that he was: *'Rochdale's greatest townsman who devoted the labours of a life and the might of an unequalled eloquence to the advancement of justice, of freedom, and of peace, looking for no earthly reward.'*

This statue was sculpted by Sir Hamo Thornycroft and unveiled in 1891 on 24th October. Originally situated in the town hall square, it was moved in 1933 to its present location where it looks out over the Esplanade. Although its fine inscription records that John Bright was almost a saintly figure, the truth seems to be more complex.

John Bright's gravestone

John Bright was born at Greenbank, Rochdale, on 16th November 1811. He was the son of Jacob Bright, a local cotton manufacturer but it is for his campaigns for Parliamentary reform, the repeal of the Corn Laws and his objection to the Crimean War that he is remembered.

As a Quaker he had grown up knowing all about prejudice. He was educated at several Quaker boarding schools, including Ackworth School near Pontefract in West Yorkshire, which was founded as a boarding school for Quaker boys and girls in 1779. He was, however, barred from attending university at Oxford or Cambridge because of his religion and, for much of his life, he was regarded as an outsider. Even his sombre Quaker coat was made fun of by his Parliamentary opponents.

He became involved in local politics in his hometown of Rochdale and led the fight to abolish the payment of tax to support the Anglican parish church.

When the Anti-Corn-Law League was formed in 1839, John became one of the founder members at the invitation of his friend, the Radical and Liberal statesman Richard Cobden. John's first wife died of tuberculosis in 1841, leaving a daughter, Helen. He was distraught but Cobden consoled him and encouraged him to prevent more deaths among the poor by continuing their campaign. Over the next few years he campaigned for free trade and from 1843 until 1847 was Member of Parliament for Durham, seeing the repeal of the Corn Laws in 1846. This opened up free trade and helped the poor to afford to feed themselves, as the removal of import tax on grain resulted in cheaper bread. The repeal was only successful because of the votes of the opposing Liberal party, of which Bright was a member, and the outcome enraged many Tories, causing the Prime Minister, Robert Peel, to resign later the same year.

In 1847 John married again, this time to Margaret Elizabeth Leatham of Wakefield, and they went on to have seven children. It was also in that year that he was returned as MP for Manchester. As a Quaker with strong views on pacifism he campaigned against the Crimean War, calling it a tragedy that caused around half a million unnecessary deaths. One famous speech of his contained the quote: 'The Angel of Death has been abroad throughout the land; you may almost hear the beating of his wings.' It was his unpopular stance against the war that caused him to lose this seat in the general election of 1857. However, just five months later, he won a by-election in Birmingham and returned to Parliament, though he remained against the war and also held the controversial view that India should be self-governing.

Another of his campaigns was for Parliamentary reform. He made a speech in 1858 in which he pointed out that only one man in six had a vote and that fewer than 200,000 voters returned more than 50% of MPs. He called for a widening of voting rights and an end to 'rotten boroughs': places where, because of the movement of population, small constituencies with only a handful of voters could return an MP whilst some industrial towns and cities with larger populations couldn't. In places where only a few individuals had a vote with no secret ballot, bribery and coercion were commonplace. John Bright pressed for the introduction of secret ballots for everyone to prevent voters being pressured by their employers or patrons into giving their vote to a chosen representative. He did not, however, believe in votes for women.

He was also opposed to slavery and condemned the Southern states of the

USA in the American Civil War, earning him the personal friendship of Abraham Lincoln. However, even though he condemned slavery, he voted against the Factory Act of 1844 as he believed that the legislation would mean lower wages for workers and would threaten Britain's export trade. The Act, which was passed, reduced the hours of work for children between eight and thirteen years of age to six and a half a day.

Bright was renowned as a skilled public speaker and he toured the country to promote his causes. Crowds would gather to hear him speak as he had a reputation for speaking his mind on a variety of issues, though he did not shout but 'he awed his listeners by the calm of his passion'.

In 1867 the Reform Act was passed by Disraeli which gave the vote to working men in the towns. When William Gladstone became Prime Minister in 1868 he appointed John Bright as President of the Board of Trade and the Liberal government went on to pass many of the other measures that Bright advocated, including a secret ballot and government-funded education. He was the first Quaker to be a cabinet minister.

The issues he campaigned for were so important to him that on two occasions he suffered nervous breakdowns from exhaustion, and poor health forced him to retire in December 1870. However, he returned to Parliament and was Chancellor of the Duchy of Lancaster from 1873 to 1874 and again from 1880 to 1882, but he resigned from the Cabinet after disagreeing with Gladstone's foreign policy. He remained the MP for Birmingham until his death on 27th March 1889.

John Bright is also associated with Llandudno in North Wales, where a local secondary school, Ysgol John Bright, is named after him. On holiday there in 1864 he stayed with his wife and son at the St George's Hotel and during a visit to the church of St Tudno on the Great Orme his five-year-old son said that when he was dead he would like to be buried there. Sadly, only a week later, the boy fell ill and died of scarlet fever and was indeed interred in the graveyard. His father returned to Llandudno to visit the grave every year until his own death.

Although he was well regarded by many, some historians remain critical of John Bright for the treatment of his own workers and his opposition to votes for women and workers' rights. Despite the glowing epitaph on his statue he remains an ambiguous figure.

SAMLESBURY

A WITCH'S GRAVE

This grave, which lies near a yew tree in the churchyard of St Leonard the Less, is sometimes called a witch's grave. It used to have long iron spikes driven through the flat gravestone as if to keep the occupant in. Legend tells that this is the grave of the wife of Tom Alker, who threatened to come back and haunt him if he married again after her death. It is said that the fractures to the stone surrounding the grave appeared when her husband planned to re-marry! It could be that the spikes were a deterrent to body snatchers. They served their purpose until 1971 when the grave was vandalised and the lower part was stolen.

STANDISH

EVA TURNER: OPERA SINGER

Eva Turner was a world-famous opera singer. Her ashes are buried in her parents' grave in the churchyard of Standish parish church.

Go into the graveyard under the gateway and take the top right-hand path; follow it around until you come to the third path on the left and the grave is on the right almost underneath the huge oak tree.

Although her father came from Wigan, Eva was born in Oldham on 10th March 1892. Her father was an engineer at the Broadway Mill on Goddard Street and Eva was a pupil at Werneth Council School until the family moved to live in Bristol when she was nine.

Eva had always shown a musical talent and her parents arranged for her to have piano lessons from the age of seven but it was when she saw a performance by the Carl Rosa Opera Company in Bristol that she became interested in a career as a singer. By the age of 11 she was having singing lessons with Dan Rootham, who also tutored Dame Clara Butt and, at the age of 13, she sang a solo in a Bristol church.

She went to the London Royal Academy of Music in 1911 and studied there for three years, after which she joined the Carl Rosa Opera Company

Eva Turner's ashes are buried in her parents' grave

and sang in the chorus before being given some small solo parts. Her debut as a soloist was in the role of the page in *Tannhäuser*, for which she was paid half a crown; she put the money in her post office savings account.

She moved on to other roles and by 1921 she had sung all over the country and was described as gifted and promising. In 1924, Ettore Panizza heard her sing in a performance of *Madame Butterfly* and asked to meet her backstage. He offered her an audition to perform with the La Scala Company in Milan. She went to sing for Arturo Toscanini and was offered a contract on the spot.

She spent the next four months learning Italian and on 16th November 1924 she sang the part of Freia in *Das Rheingold*. She was well received and though the auburn-haired Eva was only small her soprano voice was described as 'full volume with a brilliant attack at the top of the range'. Soon she was singing major roles and toured Germany, South America and the United States before coming to Covent Garden, in London, where she sang in *Aida*.

Although better known on the Continent than she was at home, Eva Turner was Britain's first international opera star. In 1926 she made headlines throughout Italy for her performance in Puccini's new opera, *Turandot*. She was offered a contract with the Teatro Regio of Turin and bought a small villa on the shores of Lake Lugano, where she enjoyed swimming in her spare time.

In June 1928, Eva sang *Turandot* at Covent Garden and received a standing ovation. It is for singing this opera with such strength and emotion that she is best known. In November the same year she sang for the first time in the USA, with the Chicago Civic Opera, as Aida, to much acclaim.

Her voice lost some of its power and stability by the late 1930s and she officially retired from singing in 1948, at the age of 50, after a final performance of *Turandot* at Covent Garden.

That August she went to New York on board the *Queen Mary* to take up the post of Visiting Professor of Voice at Oklahoma University. She only intended to stay for nine months but she remained there for the next ten years.

After this she returned to London in 1959 and became Professor of Singing at the Royal Academy of Music, where she worked until she was in her eighties, teaching singing and judging competitions.

In 1962 she was made a Dame of the British Empire and, in 1979, she was awarded an honorary doctorate of music by Manchester University. She died on 16th June 1990, at the age of 98.

When I asked the gardener at Standish church if he knew where I could find her grave he smiled and told me that many people come looking for it, including an elderly gentleman who lays flowers on the anniversary of her death every year.

STYDD

THE CHAPEL OF ST SAVIOUR: BELOW THE CHANCEL LIES A SAINT

Up a narrow track on the outskirts of the village of Ribchester is the small chapel of St Saviour, Stydd. It is a tranquil place and the simple building with its stone-flagged floor and white-washed walls is one of only a few early medieval churches in Lancashire still in use as a place of worship; monthly Sunday services are held here in the summer, as well as at Christmas, Easter and on other special occasions. Yet, in this unprepossessing place, it is believed a saint is buried. Below the chancel at Stydd chapel are thought to lie the remains of St Margaret Clitherow, also known as St Margaret of York.

STYDD

St Saviour, Stydd

There has been a place of worship here since the 12th century when deeds refer to 'the hospital of St Saviour, under Longridge and the Master and brethren also serving God there'. It could have been a monastery and perhaps a place where travellers could stay on their journey, as the term 'hospital' referred to hospitality before it became widely used as the name of a place to cure the sick. And as Ribchester, once a Roman settlement, was sited at an important road junction where the north/south crossing of the Ribble met the east/west route across the Pennines, it would seem reasonable to assume that such a resting place would have been welcome.

There is a mid 13th-century record that the Knights Hospitallers of the Order of St John of Jerusalem acquired the site from Adam, the Chaplain-Warden of the house of St Saviour at Dutton, 'together with the surrounding plough-lands, wood and moor and with rent from land in Dutton, Ribchester and elsewhere'.

By the 14th century the religious community was gone and the Knights Hospitallers rented out the land for agricultural use, although the chapel survived as the tenant was required to maintain it and to provide a chantry chaplain to sing masses for the dead. In 1501 Nicholas Talbot endowed a priest to sing for twelve months at Stydd, where his mother and father were buried. Local parish registers record that the burial ground surrounding the chapel was still in use until 1879 when burials were formally discontinued.

After the Reformation in the reign of Henry VIII, land owned by the Knights Hospitallers was forfeit to the crown and Stydd was sold to Sir Thomas Holt of Grizehurst, on condition that he paid a small stipend to a chaplain to hold occasional services in the chapel.

In 1686, Stydd Manor, including St Saviour's, was bought by a group of local gentlemen (all Roman Catholics), including James Stanford, Richard and John Shireburne of Bailey Hall and their cousins Richard and John Walmsley of Showley Hall at Clayton-le-Dale. It is possible that they purchased the chapel and burial ground to use quietly for religious purposes.

Margaret Clitherow

Margaret Clitherow was born in York in around 1553. She was the fourth child of Thomas and Jane Middleton. In 1571 she married wealthy local butcher John Clitherow, who was a widower with two young sons, and they lived in the Shambles area of the city.

The grave reputed to be the burial place of St Margaret

Although she had been raised as a Protestant and her husband also conformed to the new religion, she found 'no substance, truth or comfort' in that faith and having undertaken instruction she became a Roman Catholic in 1574. It is said that she prayed for an hour and a half every day, fasted four times a week and went regularly to confession and mass. But, the increasing religious suppression in the reign of Elizabeth I resulted in a requirement by the law that everyone attend their local parish church every Sunday and every feast day. And although her husband willingly paid her fines for non-attendance, Margaret was imprisoned on a number of occasions after recusancy was made a treasonable offence in 1576. However, she continued to hear the mass in her home and housed a schoolmaster to instruct her own and other local children in the Roman Catholic faith.

Then a law was introduced in 1585 that made it high treason, punishable by death, to aid or harbour a Roman Catholic priest. Margaret had a secret room constructed that could be accessed from the upper floor of her home, where priests and their vestments could be hidden. She also sent her son to Douai in France to study for the priesthood.

When her step-father, Henry May, became Lord Mayor of York on 15th January 1586, he pursued the policies of the Council of the North in rounding up and punishing recusants. The sheriff's men raided and searched the Clitherows' home and although the schoolmaster escaped through the secret passage, everyone else in the house was arrested, including a twelve-year-old Flemish boy who was stripped naked and threatened with a flogging if he didn't reveal the secret hiding place. The terrified boy showed them the secret room where they found enough evidence to charge Margaret with treason.

She was arrested on 10th March 1586 and accused of harbouring priests and hearing the mass. She was put on trial at the Guild Hall in York on 14th March. When she was asked for her plea, she replied: 'Having made no offence, I need no trial. I will be tried by none other than God and your consciences.'

Her refusal to plead condemned her to *peine forte et dure*, being 'pressed to death'. This consisted of the victim lying on the ground with a sharp stone under their back, their arms outstretched and their hands tied and bound to two posts. Then a wooden board or door was placed on top of them and weights were added to the board until the person was crushed to death. Margaret took fifteen agonising minutes to die, during which time she cried out for Jesus to have mercy on her.

After her death on Good Friday, her body was taken by her executioners to be buried at midnight in an obscure corner of the city where no one would find it. However, it was found six weeks later and was secretly taken away, embalmed and properly laid to rest, although one hand was removed as a holy relic. It is now kept in the Bar Convent in York.

Although there is no absolute proof of St Margaret's final burial place, it is recorded that the body was brought 'a long journey on horseback' that took a week, and as Lancashire was a place where many families stayed true to the old religion, and there was a connection between priests that Margaret had known and William Hawksworth of Mitton, it is possible that the body was brought to this area.

In 1915, historians from Stonyhurst excavated the ruins of a chantry chapel which had been attached to Bailey Hall, the home of the Shireburn family, who remained Roman Catholic. Beneath the site of the altar they discovered thirteen stone steps that led down to a crypt, laid out as a lavish shrine to a martyr; it was empty. The hall and the chantry chapel were founded in the 14th century by Robert de Cliderow, so it does not seem unreasonable that this burial place was where Margaret's body was brought. However, in later years, Richard Shireburn joined Bonnie Prince Charlie in the Jacobite Rebellion and when it was unsuccessful his estates were declared forfeit. So was the body of Margaret moved before the house was handed over?

As already mentioned, St Saviour's at Stydd had been bought by a group of gentlemen, including John Shireburne. As the Anglicans had their own church of St Wilfrid in Ribchester, they didn't need the chapel at Stydd and it is possible that it was quietly used by Roman Catholics for their worship. It is also recorded that the Anglicans in Lancashire were sympathetic to the defeated Jacobites and that the vicar of Ribchester had accepted two men 'executed for treason' for burial in his churchyard. Father Sir Walter Vavasour, who is also buried at Stydd, must have been on good terms with the vicar and it seems there would have been little to prevent the body of Margaret Clitherow being re-interred in the chapel. There is a story that says: 'She was taken a horse's journey at night and was buried; there she will remain until the church is restored to its own.' She was canonised as a saint and martyr on 25th October 1970 by Pope Paul VI. She is also the patron saint of the Catholic Women's League.

Her two sons, Henry and William, both became priests. Her daughter Anne, to whom she sent her shoes and stockings on the morning of her death so that she could follow in her footsteps, became a nun at St Ursula's, Louvain, although she was imprisoned in Lancaster Castle in 1593 for 'causes ecclesiastical'. What she was doing in the region is not recorded, but it may have been to visit her mother's grave.

Other burials at St Saviour's, Stydd

Although there is no proof that St Margaret is buried here, there are some other burials that are well recorded and not in doubt. These include the stone tombs of Sir Adam and Lady Alicia Clitheroe, dating from around 1350, which are in the floor beneath the altar. The gravestones are carved with floriated crosses and a delicate Gothic canopy; one stone bears a sword, a spear and a Latin inscription, which is now faded and worn. There is also a stone coffin tomb of great antiquity whose history is unknown and, although this is an Anglican chapel, there is the white marble gravestone of Francis Petre, of Showley Hall in Clayton-le-Dale, a Roman Catholic bishop. The Latin inscription says:

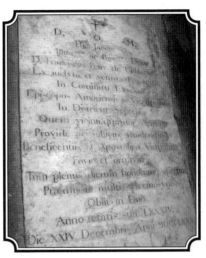

The white marble gravestone of Francis Petre

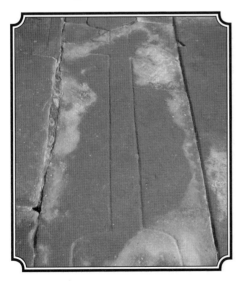

Walter Vavasour's grave

Here lies the most Illustrious and Reverend Lord Francis Petre, Of Fithlars, of an illustrious and ancient family in the county of Essex, Bishop of Amoria and Vicar Apostolic of the Northern District; which he governed with discernment and care for 24 years, being its patron and ornament by his kind acts and apostolic virtues; then full of days and good deeds, after bestowing many alms, he died in the Lord on the 24th December of the year 1775, aged 84. May he rest in peace.

There are also the graves of Richard Walmsley and Charles Ingolby, who were Catholic priests, as well as Father Sir Walter Vavasour whose burial is recorded in the parish registers: '1740, April 12th, Walter Vaviser, a reputed Romish Priest, at Stid'. His grave, just to the right of the altar, is marked by a long cross. And at the foot of the stone coffin, marked with a roughly cut cross, is said to be the burial place of St Margaret.

SUNDERLAND POINT

Sambo: a black slave

Sunderland Point lies beyond Overton near Morecambe. Sunder, or asunder, means 'apart' and at high tide this tiny village, once a thriving port, is cut off from the mainland. Just over a mile of single-track road connects it to the mainland at low tide. It is hard to imagine that ships from the West Indies and North America once docked here, plying their trade in cotton, sugar and human lives as part of the infamous 18th-century slave trade. But there are reminders, and most of the people who come here are looking for Sambo's Grave.

The well-visited grave of Sambo

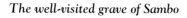

Sambo, or Samboo to give him his correct name, was a black slave who arrived at the port with his master. He was taken ill, possibly with some European disease, and died, but because he wasn't a Christian he couldn't be buried in consecrated ground, so his body was interred in land that was once behind the inn.

For a long time the grave was unmarked until some years later a retired schoolmaster discovered the story and raised money for a memorial. He also wrote the epitaph that is inscribed on the grave:

> *Full many a Sand-bird chirps upon the Sod*
> *And many a moonlight Elfin round him trips*
> *Full many a Summer's Sunbeam warms the Clod*
> *And many a teeming cloud upon him drips.*
> *But still he sleeps – till the awakening Sounds*
> *Of the Archangel's Trump now life impart*
> *Then the GREAT JUDGE his approbation founds*
> *Not on man's COLOUR but his worth of heart.*

Sentimental it may be, but it shows an awareness of changing attitudes towards people from other places. In the summer, the grave is well visited and fresh flowers have often been placed by people who come not only out of curiosity but also, maybe, with a twinge of conscience that such a thing could have happened, not just to Samboo but to countless other humans like him.

Don't give up if you can't find it at first. When you reach the hamlet and park your car on the shingle foreshore, you must follow a path that leads inland and eventually to the west shore. It is easy to miss despite being signed. The road passes several houses and the small mission church until it narrows to a path, almost overpowered by the hedgerows on either side. Eventually you will come to a barred metal gate. After going through, turn left and the grave is in a small walled enclave about 200 yards along the shore. It is always silent except for the calling of the seabirds, and the shoreline is littered with huge sea-bleached trunks of old trees that have been washed ashore on the tide. It gives the place an eerie feeling of isolation. And here lies Samboo, far from his home.

After you've walked back, instead of returning straight to your car, turn right and walk along the eastern shore. There are some lovely houses, probably built by the merchants who once traded here. Look for the row of cottages that used to be a warehouse. For almost 200 years a 'cotton tree' grew here but on New Year's Day 1998, in the fierce storm that did so much damage down the west coast, the old tree succumbed and fell. In front of the cottage where it grew is a section of the trunk, the rest of it having been taken away to be analysed. It is thought that the tree was, in fact, a kapok tree, a native of the West Indies, that could have seeded itself from some imported cargo.

Sunderland Point was built in the 18th century by Robert Lawson, a Quaker businessman. It is said that it was here the first cotton crop to enter Britain arrived but lay untouched for two years because no one knew what to do with it. Perhaps it is a good job that somebody eventually did decide to use it or the cotton towns of the north-west may never have evolved.

As the cotton towns declined, the shifting tides and changing coastline caused the decline of Sunderland as well and whilst Glasson Dock and Lancaster can still receive some shipping, the port that once overshadowed them is now almost a ghost town. A few people still live there and there is a postbox, a telephone kiosk and a tiny mission church. But it is Sambo's Grave that is the most poignant reminder of what Sunderland once was.

UP HOLLAND

A HIGHWAYMAN AND AN INDUSTRIALIST

George Lyon

Hidden in the undergrowth of the churchyard of St Thomas the Martyr at Up Holland is an insignificant flat gravestone inscribed simply: 'Nanny Lyon died 7th April 1804'. It is under the far western wall of the churchyard, amongst the shrubbery, and almost directly opposite the car park of the White Lion hotel.

It is believed that in this grave, as well as the remains of Nanny Lyon, lies the body of George Lyon, her father. He was the so-called Up Holland highwayman, who was hanged at Lancaster with his two accomplices, David

George Lyon's gravestone

Bennett and William Houghton, for a burglary they committed at Westwood Hall at Ince, near Wigan, in April 1815.

Following the burglary, George Lyon met up with a man named John McDonald who had gained his trust as a 'fence' – a dealer in stolen goods – at the Bull's Head public house in Up Holland. Lyon had boasted to McDonald that he was the 'prince of thieves' and, as time passed, locals remembered him not only as a highwayman but as a modern-day Robin Hood who took from the rich to give to the poor; but although his taking is well documented, the giving part remains unclear – unless you count the story that there were two mothers and their daughters who all bore a child fathered by George Lyon within months of each other.

McDonald agreed to buy the stolen silver from Lyon for £10 but Lyon did not know that the money was loaned by the police and McDonald was, in fact, an undercover police officer from Manchester who had been borrowed by the Wigan police as all the local officers were too well known to Lyon and his associates. By frequenting the Bull's Head for quite a while, McDonald had gained Lyon's trust and when Lyon took McDonald to his house and showed him the stolen goods, he was arrested, tried and subsequently executed for his crime.

George Lyon, despite his romanticised image, had a long history as a criminal. He had narrowly escaped hanging 30 years earlier when he had been convicted of robbery with violence in the Winstanley district of Wigan. On that occasion the death sentence was commuted to transportation to the colonies for seven years and, unusually, Lyon returned home at the end of his sentence.

His only claim to being a highwayman was when he and some accomplices robbed the Liverpool mail coach at Tawd Vale. They had persuaded the ostler at the Bull's Head to lend them some horses and they fired two shots across the coach and forced the driver to stop before robbing the passengers and returning across the fields to Up Holland where they were already settled back into the pub when the traumatised passengers arrived with their story of the hold up. As Lyon and his companions had also been in the pub earlier they claimed this as their alibi.

George Lyon continued his career as a petty thief and burglar until he was finally caught, found guilty and hanged in his mid fifties. It was usual at that time for the bodies of executed criminals to be given to local surgeons for dissection in the quest for medical knowledge, but Lyon had written a heartfelt letter to his wife on 14th April in which he begged her to arrange for his body to be taken home for burial.

As his crime did not involve the taking of human life, John Higgins, the Chief Gaoler of Lancaster Castle, agreed and also allowed Lyon to wear his best black suit and boots for his execution. Afterwards his body was collected by Simon Washington, the landlord of the Old Dog Inn in Up Holland, and brought back on a cart though a thunderstorm with torrential rain raged throughout the journey and Washington later declared that the devil had followed him every step of the way.

At Up Holland a huge crowd followed the cart to the Old Dog Inn where Lyon's body was laid out in the landlady's best parlour overnight. The next morning hundreds of people gathered outside the pub and even climbed onto the roofs of adjoining buildings to see the coffin as it was taken for burial in St Thomas's churchyard on Sunday, 23rd April 1815.

Robert Daglish

Also buried in the same churchyard and more worthy of being remembered is Robert Daglish. His grave is at the south-east corner of the church. A railed enclosure surrounds the granite tomb which bears the inscription:

In this vault lie the remains of Robert Daglish Esq, of Orrell Lodge. Who died December 26th 1865, Aged 88 years.

Robert Daglish came to Wigan from Northumbria in 1804 to work for Lord Balcarres as an engineer and manager of the Haigh Foundry and Brock Mill Forge. Here he designed a number of steam engines for pumping and

The grave of Robert Daglish

winding work in local collieries which not only led to greater efficiency but also to increased safety for the miners.

He played a major role in the development of industrial Lancashire and his greatest achievement was in 1814 after he had left Haigh to work for John Clarke as manager of the Orrell collieries on the opposite side of Wigan. Here a horse-drawn tram had to haul coal for three and a half miles from the mine to the canal quay at Crooke. As this was costing so much money as to make the colliery commercially unviable, Daglish decided to build a steam-powered locomotive based on the design of John Blenkinsop, an engineer from Leeds. Blenkinsop had invented a rack-and-pinion system in which the locomotives had a fifth wheel which engaged with a rack on one side of the rails, like many modern Swiss mountain railways. It was named the 'Yorkshire Horse' and took the place of the flesh and blood variety to transport the coal quickly, efficiently and profitably. In fact it was so successful that two more were built to the same pattern and over the 30 years that they operated at the colliery they provided a saving of £500 per year which had formerly been the stabling and feeding costs of the 14 horses; a considerable sum of money at that time.

Daglish's growing reputation as an engineer led to his appointment as a consultant on many railway projects both in this country and in America. The work of both Blenkinsop and Daglish pre-dates George Stephenson's better-known locomotives, yet Robert Daglish lies, mostly forgotten, at Up Holland, his fame eclipsed by a petty criminal.

WESTHOUGHTON

The Pretoria Pit disaster

In the cemetery adjacent to the parish church of St Bartholomew on Church Street in Westhoughton, there is a monument to honour all the men and boys who were killed in the Pretoria Pit disaster of 1910. It is also the grave of 24 miners whose bodies could not be named at the time of their burial, though eight were later identified from their clothing and personal possessions.

It was on 21st December, the darkest day of the year, at ten to eight in

The memorial to the Pretoria Pit disaster

the morning, that deep underground a roof in a tunnel fell in and set off a chain of events that culminated in a huge explosion of methane gas and coal dust. The huge explosion ripped apart Hulton Colliery, known locally as the Pretoria Pit. A local man recalls that his mother, who died at almost 100 years of age, still had vivid memories of that morning when she was eight years old. As she was getting washed in the kitchen the force of the explosion blew her off her feet. The blast was heard for miles around.

The pit employed 2,500 men and boys from the local area and on this particular morning the day shift had just begun and 898 men and boys, some as young as twelve years old, were working down the mine.

Reports of the time say that some of the miners had complained about gas and hot air in the mine and the coroner's report, prepared by a Mr Redmayne, noted that a large fall of the roof 'some twenty yards long at No.2 face of the North Plodder had not been completely removed'. There was also mention of miners seeing sparks coming from the conveyor belt switch at the No.1 face of the North Plodder which suggests that it was defective.

News of the disaster quickly spread. Men, women and children ran to help but there was little they could do as the dead and dying were brought to the surface. During the day 554 miners were rescued, but there were only two survivors from the level where the explosion occurred. A total of 344 men and boys were killed. The final conclusion of the inquest was that the roof collapse had caused the build up of gas and that a faulty lamp had ignited it.

The funerals began on Christmas Eve; there were even funerals on Christmas Day and the disaster is remembered by locals as 'Black Christmas 1910'. What people must have gone through that Christmas is unimaginable and the loss of so many men and boys must have shaped the way Westhoughton has developed over the last 100 years. One woman lost her husband and four sons, the youngest of whom was just twelve and had gone down the pit for the first time that day.

The Pretoria Pit disaster was the third largest pit accident in British history and the worst in Lancashire. The loss of life was the largest in any English coalmine. A relief fund was set up for the families and dependants, and a total of £145,000 was raised. The marble memorial which cost £200 has this inscription:

Sacred to the memory of 344 men and boys who lost their lives by an explosion at the Pretoria Pit of the Hulton Colliery Co. on the 21st December 1910, 24 of whom sleep under this monument, being unidentified at the time of burial. This monument is erected by public subscription as a token of sympathy with the widows and relatives of the victims, 171 of whom are buried in this cemetery, 45 in Wingates, 20 in Daisy Hill, 3 in the congregational churchyards, and the remainder in various burial grounds.

'Be Ye Therefore Ready Also For The Son of Man Cometh At An Hour When Ye Think Not.' St Luke XII .40

It was visited by thousands of grieving people in the days after its erection and the anniversary of the disaster is still remembered in an annual ceremony when a wreath is laid.

WHITWORTH

THE WHITWORTH DOCTORS

The graves of the Whitworth doctors can be found in the churchyard of St Bartholomew at Whitworth, set high on the hill above the village. They are near the churchyard wall, to the left as you go in from the entrance where the stocks are situated.

The dark rectangular memorial is the resting place of John Taylor and his younger brother George Taylor, who were possibly the best-known of the Whitworth doctors and whose fame spread across the whole country bringing patients both eminent and poor to the small village on the moors in the hope and expectation of a cure. The tall pink memorial nearby marks the grave of James Eastwood Taylor who was the last of the Whitworth doctors.

In the square below the church, you can see Whitworth House which is where the Taylor family lived and had their surgery. The family was in the business of healing for several generations, beginning with James Taylor who was originally a farrier and animal doctor. His two sons, John and George,

The resting place of the Whitworth doctors

also continued to treat sick animals and some believed that the horses took precedence over people, as depicted in a cartoon drawn at the time which shows John Taylor deserting Dr Thomas Thurlow, Bishop of Durham, in the middle of his treatment, to rush outside to attend to a horse. But it was their success in using their remedies to treat humans that built their reputation.

Near to the house was Doctor's Wood, where they gathered the herbs that they used to make their remedies. These were boiled up and prepared in the kitchen by Mrs George Taylor and included a herbal drink to purify the blood, a liniment called Red Rubbing Bottle, a black salve and copious quantities of snuff made from a rare woodland plant *Asarabacca Europaeum*, which grew locally.

It was with snuff, made from the powdered dried leaves of this plant, that

John Taylor is reputed to have cured the Princess Elizabeth, daughter of George III and Queen Charlotte. The king had sent for John after he had cured a dying duchess, who was a lady-in-waiting to the queen, by lancing an abscess. The princess was suffering from constant pain in her head, probably a sinus condition, and the doctor administered snuff, which set off such a sneezing fit that her family became quite alarmed. 'Let her sneeze,' said the doctor, 'that is the very thing that will do her good.' And the remedy completely relieved the princess of her complaint.

Although the better known of the two doctors was John, it was George, his younger brother, who was granted a licence, issued by the Bishop of Chester, to practise 'the Several Arts or professions of Physic and Chirurgery within and throughout the Diocese of Chester'. The doctors treated anyone who came, on a 'first come first seen' basis, making no exceptions for the rich and titled who had to sit and wait with the rest. They charged everyone the same fee of 18 pence a week, though the rich often gave donations and if someone was too poor to afford the fee they were never asked for the money. In fact there was a subscription box for the support of those who were too poor to pay for their treatment and John Taylor, as well as contributing himself, often took the box around to his wealthier patients and solicited contributions from them.

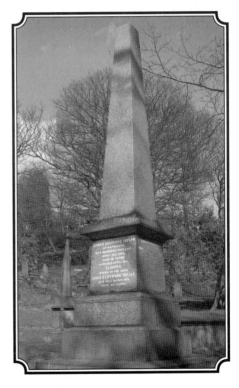

The memorial to James Eastwood Taylor, the last of the Whitworth doctors

Patients varied from people who lived locally, or came to lodgings on the outskirts of the village, to rich gentry who travelled the length of the country and stayed, sometimes for many months, at the local inn, the Red Lion, whilst they underwent their treatment.

Writing in 1819, William Howitt describes a visit to Whitworth: 'All about the village were wretched invalids walking, some with patched faces, some with an arm or a leg bound fast to a board – I suppose in order to straiten them; some with splints on their arm, shewing that they had been broken; others moving along slowly like spectres, in the lowest state of physical exhaustion, and others groaning inwardly as they passed, evidently from the tortures they were undergoing from the keen.'

The 'keen' to which he refers was a caustic substance, which came in two varieties, red and white, that was used to remove cancers. The doctors specialised in the cure of cancers, as well as setting broken bones and straightening limbs. William Howitt goes on to record the stories of two women patients. One bore the pain of the 'keen' for two to three hours daily and her cancer was successfully removed. Another woman, with breast cancer, travelled over a 100 miles to see Dr John Taylor, who, after examining her told her to return home as there was no hope that she could be cured. But she insisted that he tried, saying that she could bear any pain and was willing for the treatment to be kill or cure. 'Thou art a brave lass,' said John. 'I will try.' The lady stayed in Whitworth for six months and endured excruciating pain, but finally she was cured and lived for another 30 years.

Another patient was the wife of a nobleman who had been 'startled by a sudden fright, had fallen and from that time had been unable to put a foot on the ground'. John Taylor insisted that she try to walk, and as she struggled to stand, leaning on her husband, he ran up behind her and pushed her hard with his knee. The nobleman was incensed at this insult to his wife, but the doctor told him he was a fool. 'Let the woman try to walk again,' he said. And when she was eventually persuaded to try, she found that she could. The doctor explained that the woman had dislocated her hip and that he had returned the joint to its correct position.

Although neither of the doctors seems to have had much time for fawning over the gentry, the caring nature of John Taylor, as well as people's faith in his ability, is illustrated by the story of a local man who brought two pitiable horses to the doctor. The man made his living by carting coal and although the two horses were worn out he couldn't afford to buy another, so he asked the doctor if he could take the two horses and make one good one out of them. John told him to come back in a fortnight and when he did he presented him with a young and healthy horse of his own, but the man was not entirely satisfied. After examining the horse he said, 'It's a wall'd eyed 'un[1] I canna abide a wall'd eyed 'un.' The doctor told him that he should have mentioned it before and it was too late to alter it now and the man went off believing that the horse was a healthy compound of the two sickly ones he had brought. Though whether Dr Taylor did it for the sake of the man or the sake of the horses will never be known.

John Taylor died on 26th January 1802, aged 62, and his brother George died two years later. James Taylor (1768–1826), the son of John, continued the practice and was succeeded by his son George and then James Eastwood Taylor, who lived until 1876 and was the last of the Whitworth doctors.

WOODPLUMPTON

Meg Shelton – the Fylde Witch

In the churchyard of St Anne's at Woodplumpton, to the left of the path just beyond the church, you will see a large boulder that could have been carried to the area on a glacier during the Ice Age. Under this boulder is buried the body of Margery Hilton who died in 1705. She was found dead in her cottage, crushed between a barrel and a wall.

She is more commonly known by the name Meg Shelton and is better known as the Fylde Witch. Meg had lived at Cuckoo Hall, near Wesham, in a cottage that was described as a wretched hovel, where she subsisted on a diet of boiled groats mixed with parsley and thyme and whatever else she could steal. She later moved to a cottage at Catforth, where she lived for the rest of her life. Legend tells that she had made a bet with the landlord that if she could turn herself into a hare and race the landlord's dogs from Wesham to Catforth and arrive first, the cottage would be hers. Her only stipulation

[1](a horse with blue eyes or blue, ringed with white, rather than the customary brown eyes)

was that his ferocious black dog should not be sent after her. However, the landlord went back on his word and freed the black dog which caught up with Meg just outside the cottage door and managed to nip her on the heel before she got inside, leaving her with a permanent limp.

Other tales are told about Meg's ability to turn herself into a variety of living creatures, as well as taking the shape of seemingly ordinary household implements – such as a broom, for example. One story relates that a miller at Singleton suspected her of stealing his corn. Night after night he watched and saw her going into the mill, but when he rushed across to confront her there was no one there. So one day he carefully counted how many sacks of grain he had stored and when he ran in that night to a seemingly empty barn he counted them again and found there was one extra. He seized a pitchfork and plunged it into each sack in turn until, with a squeal of rage

The boulder that marks the resting place of Meg Shelton

and her arm bleeding from the wound, Meg seized a nearby broom and flew off into the night.

Another day, a local farmer saw her flying low over his cows with a jug in her hand, but by the time he reached the field he could only find an old woman grazing her goose. But then he caught sight of a bead of milk on the goose's beak. He kicked the goose which shattered into the fragments of a jug in a pool of milk and an angry Meg flew off over the hedge on her broomstick.

Because Margery Hilton had been baptised and had never been 'examined as a witch' it was grudgingly agreed that after her death she had the right to a Christian burial in holy ground. Many of the locals were unhappy about this so, as a compromise, she was buried by torchlight on the night of 2nd May 1705.

Legend tells that soon after her burial, Meg clawed her way back to the surface and when she was buried a second time, she scratched her way out again. So a priest from nearby Cottam Hall came to exorcise the place where she lay. Afterwards she was re-buried for a third time, head down, so that if she began to dig again she would only dig herself deeper in. The grave was then topped by the boulder you can still see today and locals were reassured that she couldn't escape. Though that doesn't explain why, one day in 1933, a young boy who was visiting the Fylde with his family, went into the church ahead of the adults and moments later came running out, terrified, saying that an old woman dressed in 'funny clothes' had chased him.

There is also an old ritual associated with the grave. You must walk around it three times then stand on the stone. Look north, then east, then south and finally west. Then you make a wish and run round the church three times, but if you see the devil through the keyhole of the church door, you must run away even faster! It seems that the Fylde Witch still has power over the locals.

LANCASHIRE Who Lies Beneath?

INDEX